Baking with
Tiny Tots

NOTES

To measure a dry ingredient, such as sugar and most flour, place it in a measuring cup or spoon and level it with the straight edge of a knife or spatula. For cake flour, sift it to make it lighter. For brown sugar, press it firmly into the measuring cup or spoon. If butter or another shortening does not come in a wrapper with tablespoon or cup measurements, measure it in the the same way as for brown sugar. To measure liquids in a measuring jug, check the liquid against the mark at eye level.

All eggs used in the recipes are medium. Ovens should be preheated to the specified temperature convection.

This book includes dishes made with nuts. It is advisable for those with known allergic reactions to nuts and nut derivatives and those who may be potentially vulnerable to these allergies, such as pregnant and nursing mothers, invalids, the elderly, babies, and children, to avoid foods made with nuts. It is also prudent to check the labels of commercially-prepared ingredients for the possible inclusion of nut derivatives.

Children should be supervised by an adult at all times when cooking or baking. The tasks that can be performed at a particular age or stage in their development will differ from child to child.

While the advice and information in this book are believed to be accurate, neither the author nor the publisher can accept any legal responsibility for any illness sustained while following the advice in this book.

First published in Great Britain in 2007 by
Hamlyn, a division of Octopus Publishing Group Ltd.
2–4 Heron Quays, London E14 4JP.

Copyright © Octopus Publishing Group Ltd. 2007

641.815
JOHN

ISBN-13: 978-0-600-60972-8
ISBN-10: 0-600-60972-3

A CIP catalogue record for this book is available from the British Library

Printed and bound in China

10 9 8 7 6 5 4 3 2 1

JUL 1 1 2007

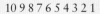

Becky Johnson

Baking with Tiny Tots

Over 50 easy recipes for young children to enjoy making

hamlyn

Contents

Introduction

Whoever said never to work with children or animals has obviously not tried baking with little ones because it is a joy to cook with even the tiniest of tots. Okay, so it may get a little messy, but the results are worth it. Children's energy and enthusiasm for cooking are an inspiration, and any doubts that some of the trickier tasks, such as piping, kneading, or rubbing in, are beyond their young years are often dispelled by displays of earnest concentration, determination, and exuberant completion of the task. That they are then able to eat the results of their labor is invariably met with wonder and joy.

Children like to feel that they contribute to family life. They want to be helpful and do what they see you doing. Baking is one way that they can produce real results, ones that everyone can enjoy and appreciate.

My seven-year-old daughter is genuinely excited by other people's birthdays and now she insists on making them a cake. This is always received with rapturous delight, making her truly proud.

This book is full of child-friendly ideas for food that you and your little ones can bake together, and all the recipes have been tested on children. A family baking session is a lovely way to spend time together. In this book, you'll find ideas for a quick lunch or a snack-time cake through to edible Christmas decorations and party treats. Together, you can make the food for a picnic or their lunch box, delicious gifts for friends and relatives, and irresistible snacks for the cookie jar.

Additive-free food Baking at home also gives control back to us parents over what our children eat. The kids can still enjoy sweet treats but without the long list of additives most of us know little about and fear may harm their growing bodies. Instead of giving your children a store-bought cake, open their young minds to the wonderful variety of textures, smells, and tastes of home baking. Show them where their food comes from and how they can combine different ingredients to make yummy cookies, cakes, and pastries. With just a little encouragement, a lifelong interest in real food and cooking may easily be sparked at this tender age.

Be relaxed First baking experiences need to be fun. The recipes in this book are easy and quick. They don't require long attention spans, but be prepared to step in if your child is wavering before completing the whole tray of cookies! I found my daughter was always happy to sit and lick out the bowl, or "help" by washing the dishes in a sink full of bubbles, while I finished the recipe.

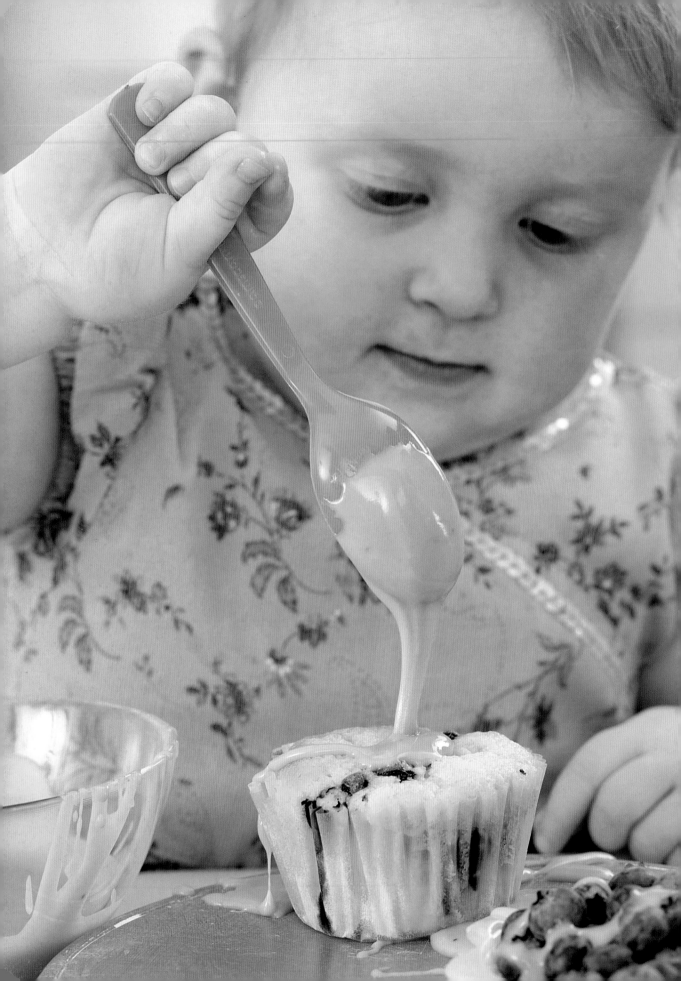

The important thing when cooking with little children is to allow a lot of time—children hate being hurried—and not to worry too much about the look of the results! It's the time spent creating something together that's important.

Learning is fun Children learn a huge amount from cooking without even realizing it. First, there's the exposure to cookbooks full of recipes. From these they learn that the written word provides information that can be used to make things. They also see photos of other children doing things that they will then want to try themselves. Second, there's the coordination required to measure out ingredients, to mix, spoon out, beat, and spread. Next, measuring introduces children to the concepts of numbers, volume, and accuracy. Finally, there's the chemistry involved in the baking itself—the transforming effect of heat on food.

Encouraging independence Because cooking is an activity that uses all of the senses, it totally absorbs children. It gives them a sense of achievement and confidence as they try new actions by themselves. As they become older and more capable, your children will be able to make their favorite foods by themselves, and developing a familiarity with food and cooking at a young age may give them the confidence to be more creative in the kitchen in later life.

We live in an age where many people don't know how to cook, and rely heavily on convenience foods and commercially-prepared meals. Encouraging your children to cook for themselves and to learn how to transform sets of ingredients into cakes, cookies and eventually casseroles and roast dinners can only be a good thing for them in adulthood and will hopefully encourage them to pass these skills onto their own children in time.

Shopping for ingredients Not only do children learn about food and cooking when in the kitchen, but taking them shopping for the ingredients you're going to use is a learning experience, too. Whether they're sitting in the shopping cart, or walking along beside you in the supermarket, involve your children in the food-shopping process. Teach them how to locate items along the aisles, get them to help you track down specific ingredients, and explain their uses and their origin if possible. It all helps spark children's interest and may even encourage fussy eaters to try unfamiliar foods once back at home.

What can your child do? Children can—and indeed like to—help you in the kitchen from the time they are old enough to stand on a chair and reach the countertop. Covering their hands with yours and letting them think they are cutting butter or spreading frosting gives them a huge thrill and costs you nothing but patience. Even the smallest child should be able to use a cookie cutter to cut shapes out of dough. Children develop at different rates but between the ages of three and six you'll find they can wash fruit and vegetables for you, stir ingredients in a bowl, and, under direction, add ingredients to the bowl. Over-sixes will be able to use measuring spoons, measure liquids into a jug, and beat ingredients with a whisk.

Recipe steps that young children should find particularly easy to carry out are marked with a chef's hat. Adult supervision is recommended at all times.

Tips for kneading dough The best bit of kneading is that it doesn't really need to be done in any specific way, so you can throw the dough down on the table and punch it, pull it, and twist it. Children are very good at kneading dough, but if they need some instruction, tell them to grab the side of the dough nearest to them and, holding onto it, push the other side of the dough down and away from them with the palm of their hand. Then lift the far edge up and over into the center. Now give the dough a quarter turn and knead again as before. Do this for at least 10 minutes, or until the dough becomes smooth textured, elastic, and no longer sticky. Children can become tired kneading dough, so be prepared to step in and finish the job.

Getting started First choose your recipe, bearing in mind the age and ability of your child. Remember that cooking with a little one takes much longer than cooking on your own, so make sure you have plenty of time to complete the recipe. Collect together all the necessary ingredients and equipment before you start so you can check you've got what you need. It's infuriating to have to abandon a recipe halfway through cooking because you're missing an ingredient you thought you had. It will also cause intense disappointment on the part of your assistant chef!

What you'll need You don't *have* to buy any special equipment in order to bake with children, but certain items will make life easier for them and may mean they enjoy the baking experience more.

- **step-up stool** It's worth investing in a child's step-up stool or a child-sized chair so that your child can see above the countertop and/or have a low table that they can work on. Alternatively, they could sit on a clean floor or on a plastic sheet or tablecloth.

- **apron** A little apron is a treat for small cooks. A wipe-clean one will make it particularly easy to avoid splashes and keep your little one clean. A cheaper alternative is to use an old shirt (check out the thrift shop) or even a raincoat!

- **a set of measuring cups** These come in different sizes, from ¼ cup to 1 cup. Remember to use the back of a knife or spatula to level dry ingredients, such as sugar.

- **small wooden spoon** A small wooden spoon is child-friendly and makes beating and mixing much easier for very little ones.

- **a set of measuring spoons** These are useful for accurately measuring ingredients in whole and fractions of teaspoons and tablespoons. Fill the spoons level—a rounded measure could almost double the amount of ingredient required! Don't use everyday spoons as their designs, depths, and shapes vary.

- **plastic measuring jugs and bowls** Plastic equipment is obviously better than glass for children's use, in case of clumsy hands.

Safety first Small children must always be supervised in the kitchen. Teach them basic hygiene rules from an early age, as well as tell them about the potential dangers posed by hot ovens, full saucepans, and sharp knives.

- **hygiene** Always wash hands before starting to cook and make sure surfaces are clean. Tie back long hair and don an apron or coverall.

- **ovens and cooktops** Take special care when opening oven doors in front of expectant little ones and make sure they stand well back so they don't get blasted by very hot air. Always use oven mitts. Also be especially wary of recently turned off but still very hot burners. Use the back burners of the hob when working with small children so there's no temptation to grab saucepan handles from below to see what's cooking.

- **sharp knives** It's great to involve young children in the clearing-up process—to them it's just as much fun as the cooking and you can establish good working practices from the start. But make it a rule never to place any sharp knives or food processor blades in the sink, where they can easily be hidden by soap bubbles. Instead, rinse them as you work and place them straight back into the knife rack or into a drawer, well out of harm's way.

Storage If you don't eat them all within hours of baking them, most of the cakes and cookies in this book will keep for 2–3 days in an airtight container, such as a cake container or cookie jar. If you want to prepare in advance or decide you only want to finish off half the quantity you have made, unfrosted cakes and uncooked cookie dough can be placed in plastic food storage bags and frozen for up to a month.

1

A piece of cake

Lemon sand castles

Makes 6
Preparation time 15 minutes
Cooking time 20 minutes

Equipment

6-hole muffin pan • wax baking paper • pencil • scissors • paper towel • large mixing bowl • wooden spoon • small mixing bowl • sifter or seive • dessert spoon • baking sheet • knife • cooling rack • teaspoon

Ingredients

½ cup (1 stick) butter or margarine, softened, plus extra for greasing
½ cup superfine sugar
2 eggs
⅓ cup cornmeal (ordinary or quick-cook variety)
1 cup all-purpose flour
grated rind of a lemon
2 tablespoons plain yogurt

For the frosting

2 cups powdered sugar, sifted
juice of ½ an unwaxed lemon
pinch of saffron (strands or powdered), soaked in 1 tablespoon boiling water
flags, candy, or cake decorations

Planted with toothpick flags, these little lemon cakes look like sand castles and even have an authentic "gritty" texture from the cornmeal.

What to do

1   Preheat the oven to 350°F. To line the bottom of the dariole molds, place them on a piece of wax paper and allow your child to draw around them with a pencil. Then, if the little hands have mastered scissors, cut around the circles and place one in the bottom of each mold.

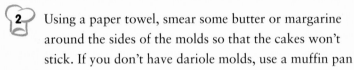

2   Using a paper towel, smear some butter or margarine around the sides of the molds so that the cakes won't stick. If you don't have dariole molds, use a muffin pan and prepare the same way.

3   After helping you measure out the butter or margarine and the sugar into a large mixing bowl, let your child mix them together with a wooden spoon until really creamy.

4   Break the eggs carefully into a small bowl and add them to the large bowl one at a time, stirring in well. Finally, sift in the flour, add all the other ingredients, and stir together until you have a smooth mixture.

5   Help your child to use a dessert spoon to spoon the mixture into the prepared molds or pan until they are about two-thirds full.

6   Place all the molds together on a baking sheet and bake for 20 minutes, or until golden on top.

7   Slide a knife around the edge of the molds to loosen the cakes and then tip onto a cooling rack and let cool.

8   Meanwhile, your child can stir together the ingredients to make the frosting. Drizzle over the cakes with a teaspoon then decorate with flags, candy or cake decorations.

Yummy stars

Dark, moist gingerbread cut into stars and drizzled with a bright white glacé icing and sugar stars or little silver decorations.

What to do

1   Place the baking pan on a sheet of parchment paper and have your child draw around it with a pencil.

2   Cut out the square and place it in the base of the pan. Preheat the oven to 300°F. Put the molasses in a small saucepan and heat gently.

3   Put the butter and sugar in the large mixing bowl and help your child to beat them together until creamy.

4   Add the molasses and egg and stir to combine. Sift in the flour and ginger and stir in. Scrape into the prepared pan and bake for 30 minutes, or until a skewer inserted in the middle comes out clean.

5   Let the cake stand in the pan to cool and then tip out and, using a star cutter, help your child to cut the cake into 15 star shapes. Eat the trimmings!

6   Meanwhile, make the icing by stirring together the ingredients in a small bowl. Drizzle the icing over the stars with a teaspoon and then add the silver decorations.

Makes 15 stars
Preparation time 20 minutes
Cooking time 30 minutes

Equipment
large baking pan, 12 inches square •
parchment paper • **pencil** • **scissors** •
small saucepan • **large mixing bowl** •
wooden spoon • **sifter or seive** •
spatula • **thin wooden or metal skewer** •
star-shaped cutter • **dessert spoon** •
small mixing bowl • **teaspoon**

Ingredients
1 tablespoon molasses
**½ cup (1 stick), plus 2 tablespoons butter
   or margarine, softened**
¾ cup dark brown sugar
1 egg
2½ cups all-puurpose flour
2 teaspoons ground ginger
⅔ cup plain yogurt

For the icing
1 tablespoon lemon juice (or water)
2 cups powdered sugar, sifted
1 tablespoon warm water
edible silver decorations

Rock cakes

Makes 12
Preparation time 15 minutes
Cooking time 15–20 minutes

Equipment
2 large baking sheets • **parchment baking paper** • **scissors** • **large mixing bowl** • **sifter or seive** • **wooden spoon** • **dessert spoon** • **cooling rack**

Ingredients
½ cup (1 stick) butter, softened
2 cups all-purpose flour
½ teaspoon cinnamon (optional)
grated rind of an orange
½ cup light brown sugar, plus extra for sprinkling
½ cup mixed dried fruit (if your child is not keen on the store-bought mixes, you can make your own version by chopping dried apricots, glacé cherries, and citrus peel)
1 egg, beaten
drop of milk (optional)

Contrary to their name, these little cakes are soft and sweet, but they do look like they are rugged rocks.

What to do

1   Help your child to cut large pieces of the parchment paper to fit the baking sheets while you preheat the oven to 400°F.

 2   Put the butter into a large bowl, sift in the flour and cinnamon, if using, and tell your child to put their hands in the bowl and rub the flour and butter together until the butter is all broken up and covered in flour and the mixture resembles bread crumbs.

3   Add the orange rind, sugar, fruit, and egg, and stir it all together with a wooden spoon (this stage is too sticky for hands to manage). Add a little milk if the mixture is too crumbly.

 4   Use a dessert spoon to put untidy mounds of the mixture onto the baking sheets.

5   Sprinkle the tops of the cakes with a little more light brown sugar, then bake for 15–20 minutes, or until golden brown on the edges.

6   Remove from the oven and allow to cool for 15 minutes on the tray, then transfer to a cooling rack.

Blueberry and apple muffins

Quick and easy, these ingredients could be measured out, placed in two separate bowls the night before, then put together and baked for a special breakfast—a Mother's Day treat perhaps.

What to do

1   Show your child how to put the paper liners into the muffin pan while you preheat the oven to 400°F.

2   Divide the ingredients into two large mixing bowls: all the dry ingredients (sifted flour, baking soda, and sugar) in one bowl and all the wet (melted butter, yogurt, milk, egg, blueberries, and apple) in another.

3   Ask your child to stir the ingredients in their separate bowls until well mixed.

4   Help your child pour the wet ingredients into the dry. It is important to mix quickly and minimally—as with all muffins, it's best to have a lumpy mixture that will be soft and rise rather than a well-mixed one that will not rise and be tough.

5   Quickly spoon the mixture into the prepared liners so that each is about three-quarters full. Have your child sprinkle each with a little more of the sugar. Bake for 20 minutes, or until risen and golden.

6   Remove the muffins from the oven and let them cool a little in the pan before transferring to a cooling rack. Eat warm or cold.

Makes 12
Preparation time 15 minutes
Cooking time 20 minutes

Equipment
12 paper muffin liners • 12-cup muffin pan • sifter or sieve • 2 large mixing bowls • wooden spoon • dessert spoon • cooling rack

Ingredients
¾ cup all-purpose flour
½ teaspoon baking soda
½ cup soft light brown sugar, plus extra for sprinkling
½ cup butter (1 stick), melted
½ cup plain yogurt
½ cup milk
1 egg, beaten
1⅓ cups blueberries
1 apple, cored, peeled, and diced small

"Lamingtons"

Makes 12
Preparation time 20 minutes
Cooking time 15–20 minutes

Equipment

2 x 2-lb loaf pans • wax paper • large
mixing bowl • wooden spoon, fork, or
handheld electric mixer • sifter or sieve •
cooling rack • medium-sized mixing
bowl • small bowl • saucer • large
serrated knife • rubber spatula • board
or plate

Ingredients

½ cup (1 stick) butter or margarine,
   softened
½ cup sugar
2 eggs
1¾ cups all-purpose flour
1 teaspoon vanilla extract
about 3 tablespoons milk

For the icing

4 tablespoons butter or margarine,
   softened
1½ cups powdered sugar, sifted
1 tablespoon cocoa powder
2–3 tablespoons preboiled warm water
½–⅔ cup shredded coconut
1–2 tablespoons milk (optional)

For the filling

4 tablespoons raspberry
   or strawberry jam

As Australian as kangaroos, these jam-filled
sponge cakes taste exceedingly good and are
fun and messy to make!

What to do

1   Preheat the oven to 350°F, and grease and line the loaf
    pans with wax paper.

2   Put the butter and sugar in a large mixing bowl and, using
    a wooden spoon, fork, or electric mixer, mash them
    together until light and creamy.

3   Beat in the eggs, one at a time. Sift in the flour, and add
    the vanilla and just enough milk to combine to a soft
    dropping consistency.

4   Spoon into the prepared pans and smooth the top. Bake
    for 15–20 minutes, or until golden brown and springy to
    the touch. Remove from the pan and cool on a rack.

5   Meanwhile, make the icing. Beat the butter and sugar
    together until light and creamy. In a separate small bowl,
    mix the cocoa and warm water together and then add to
    the butter mix and beat until smooth.

6   Tip the shredded coconut into a saucer. Slice the cakes in
    half crossways through the middle and spread the bases
    with jam. Replace the tops and cut each cake into
    6 equal-sized squares.

7   Dip all sides of the squares first into the chocolate icing
    and then into the coconut. Set onto a board or plate to
    dry completely before serving (if towards the end the icing
    becomes too thick, simply thin it down with a spoonful
    or two of milk).

Banana muffins

A great recipe for little ones to make because the secret to a good muffin is not to mix it too well. Lumpy is good!

What to do

1. Ask your child to place the paper liners in the pan while you preheat the oven to 350°F.

2. Put the butter, honey and milk in the small pan and place on a low heat until melted.

3. Show your child how to mash the bananas with a fork in the small bowl. Sift the flour and baking soda into a large bowl and mix together.

4. Pour the melted butter mixture into the mashed bananas and mix, then tip into the flour and mix together with a wooden spoon. At this stage tell your child not to over-mix—just a couple of stirs will do or the muffins will be tough and flat.

5. Without delay, spoon the mixture into the muffin liners so that each is about two-thirds full. Bake for 20–25 minutes, until risen and golden.

6. Remove from the oven and let cool in the pan for 5 minutes, then transfer the muffins in their liners to a cooling rack.

7. While the muffins are cooling, make the caramel icing. Sift the powdered sugar into a bowl, add the caramel sauce, and mix together with enough preboiled warm water, about 2–3 tablespoons, to make a thick but spoonable icing. When cool, ask your child to blob the icing on top of each muffin with a teaspoon and let it run. Stick a banana chip to the wet icing to decorate.

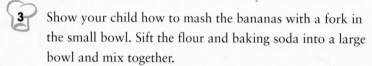

Makes 6
Preparation time 15 minutes
Cooking time 20–25 minutes

Equipment
6 paper muffin liners • 6-cup muffin pan • small saucepan • fork • small mixing bowl • sifter or sieve • large mixing bowl • wooden spoon • dessert spoon • cooling rack • teaspoon

Ingredients
2 tablespoons butter
2 tablespoons clear honey
2 tablespoons milk
2 large very ripe bananas
1¼ cups all-purpose flour
½ teaspoon baking soda

For the icing
1½ cups powdered sugar
1 teaspoon caramel sauce
2–3 tablespoons preboiled warm water
dried banana chips, to decorate

Rainbow cupcakes

These little orange-scented cakes are iced and dipped into sprinkles.

What to do

1. Show your child how to place the cake liners in the muffin pan while you preheat the oven to 350°F.

2. Put the butter, sugar, orange rind, and vanilla extract into the mixing bowl and help your child beat them together until creamy.

3. Add the egg and beat the mixture again, then sift in the flour and stir it in. Spoon the mixture into the cake liners with a teaspoon so they are three-quarters full.

4. Bake the cakes for 10–15 minutes, or until they are risen and golden. Remove from the oven and let cool for a few minutes before transferring to a cooling rack and letting them cool completely.

5. Meanwhile, make the icing by sifting the powdered sugar into a bowl and stirring it together with the orange juice.

6. When the cakes are cool, drizzle the icing over them with a teaspoon or dip them into the icing to cover. Pour the sprinkles into a saucer and dip in the iced cakes. Let them set.

Makes 24 mini cakes or 12 cupcakes
Preparation time 20 minutes
Cooking time 10–15 minutes

Equipment
24 small cake liners or 12 cupcake liners • 24- or 12-cup muffin pan • large mixing bowl • wooden spoon • sifter or sieve • teaspoon • cooling rack • saucer

Ingredients
4 tablespoons butter or margarine, softened
¼ cup sugar
grated rind of an unwaxed orange
few drops vanilla extract
1 egg
½ cup all-purpose flour

For the icing
1½ cups powdered sugar
2 tablespoons orange juice
sprinkles or other cake decorations

Flower cupcakes

Makes 12
Preparation time 10 minutes
Cooking time 15–20 minutes

Equipment
12 paper muffin liners • 12-cup muffin pan • food processor (or mixing bowl and wooden spoon) • dessert spoon • cooling rack • sharp knife • small bowls for coloring the icing • teaspoons

Ingredients
½ cup (1 stick) butter or margarine, softened
½ cup sugar
2 eggs
1 cup all-purpose flour
few drops vanilla extract
2 tablespoons milk

For the icing
1 lb package instant royal icing
food coloring (one or more colors, as desired)
sugar or rice paper flowers or other cake decorations

Children love to ice and decorate these pretty, light-as-fairies cupcakes.

What to do

 1   Ask your child to put the paper liners in the muffin pan while you preheat the oven to 350°F.

2   If you have a food processor, put all the ingredients except the milk into it and mix until smooth, then add the milk a little at a time down the funnel of the food processor until you have a mixture that is a soft, dropping consistency. Alternatively, follow steps 2–3 of the Lamington recipe on page 22 for the manual method.

 3   Help your child to spoon mixture into the liners.

4   Bake the cakes for 15–20 minutes, or until they are golden and springy to the touch. Let cool for a few minutes in the pan, then transfer to a cooling rack. When cool, slice off the pointy tops with a sharp knife.

5   Make up the royal icing as directed on the package and then divide into small bowls, one for each choice of color.

6   To color the royal icing, first cover any porous work surface with a plastic cloth or newspaper, or work on a metal draining board. Pour a few drops of coloring into the lid of the bottle, then ask your child to add the coloring to the first bowl of icing, drop by drop. Add different coloring to the other bowls of icing if you want.

 7   Mix the icing well and let your child spoon the icing onto the cakes and decorate to their taste.

Coconut and raspberry cupcakes

Makes 12
Preparation time 15 minutes
Cooking time 20 minutes

Equipment
12 paper muffin liners • **12-cup muffin pan** • **small saucepan** • **large mixing bowl** • **sifter or sieve** • **wooden spoon** • **large measuring jug** • **cooling rack**

Ingredients
½ cup (1 stick) butter
½ cup shredded coconut
2 cups powdered sugar
¾ cup all-purpose flour
4 egg whites
1½ cups fresh raspberries

These delicious cupcakes are studded with clusters of fresh raspberries.

What to do

 1 Show your child how to place the paper liners in the muffin pan while you preheat the oven to 350°F.

2 Put the butter in a small saucepan and melt over a low heat. Meanwhile, help your child to sift the flour and icing sugar into a large mixing bowl, add the coconut, and stir together.

3 Add the egg whites and stir together, then add the melted butter and stir again until combined into a thick batter.

4 Tip the batter into a measuring jug and help your child pour the batter into the prepared muffin liners, filling each one about half full.

 5 Ask you child to place a few raspberries on the top of each cake.

6 Bake the cakes for 20 minutes, or until they are golden and springy to the touch. Remove them from the oven and let cool for a few minutes in the pan before transferring them to a cooling rack.

Mud pies

This recipe is a little bit tricky in that it needs a lot of whisking, but it's worth the effort for the rich, gooey mud mixture and resulting irresistible pies.

Makes 12
Preparation time 20 minutes
Cooking time 15 minutes

Equipment

12-cup muffin pan • **12 paper muffin liners** • **small saucepan** • **medium heatproof bowl** • **large mixing bowl, preferably with a pouring lip** • **hand-held electric mixer (or food processor with whisk attachment)** • **sifter or sieve** • **large metal spoon** • **cooling rack** • **small sieve**

Ingredients

7 ounces semisweet chocolate, broken into small pieces
¾ cup (1½ stick), plus 1 tablespoon butter
3 eggs
6 tablespoons sugar
1 cup all-purpose flour
2 tablespoons cocoa powder or icing sugar to decorate (optional)

What to do

1   Ask your child to put the paper liners in the muffin pan while you preheat the oven to 325°F.

2   Fill the small saucepan with 2 inches of water, bring to a boil, then lower the heat so that the water is simmering.

3   Put the chocolate pieces and butter in the heatproof bowl and place over the simmering water in the saucepan until melted, then stir together gently.

4   Put the eggs and sugar in the large mixing bowl and help your child to beat with the electric mixer for a full 5 minutes, until very light and foamy. Alternatively, this could be done more easily in a food processor with a whisk attachment.

5   Have your child sift the flour into the egg foam. Add the chocolate mixture and show your child how to fold them together with a large metal spoon, being careful not to knock all the air out of the mixture.

6   Help your child to pour or spoon the "mud" into the muffin liners so that each is about half full, then bake for 15 minutes.

7   When they are cooked, remove them from the oven and let cool for 5–10 minutes in the pan before transferring them to a cooling rack.

8   If you wish, your child can put a tablespoon or so of cocoa powder or icing sugar into a small sieve and dust the cakes to decorate.

Chocolate teddies

The easiest one-bowl cake mixture made with milk and white chocolate chips. Here we've decorated them as teddies, but let your child use their own decorative ideas.

What to do

1. Show your child how to place the paper liners in the muffin pan while you set the oven to 350°F.

2. Put the butter, sugar, and vanilla extract in the mixing bowl and help your child beat them together until creamy.

3. Add the eggs and beat the mixture again, then sift in the flour and stir it in. Finally, stir in the chocolate chips. Spoon the mixture into the cake liners with a dessert spoon so that they are three-quarters full.

4. Bake for 10–15 minutes, or until risen and golden. Remove from the oven and let cool for a few minutes before transferring to a cooling rack and letting cool completely.

5. Meanwhile, make the chocolate frosting by sifting the icing sugar and cocoa into a bowl, adding the butter, then beating the ingredients together until smooth.

6. When the cakes are cool, spread them with the icing. Use a fork to make the icing look like fur and then decorate them, making eyes, ears, and a nose.

Makes 12
Preparation time 20 minutes
Cooking time 10–15 minutes

Equipment
12 cup cake liners • 12-cup muffin pan • large mixing bowl • wooden spoon • sifter or sieve • dessert spoon • cooling rack • medium mixing bowl • fork

Ingredients
½ cup (1 stick) butter, softened
7 tablespoons sugar
few drops vanilla extract
2 eggs
¾ cup all-purpose flour
⅓ cup milk chocolate chips
⅓ cup white chocolate chips

For the chocolate frosting
4 tablespoons butter, softened
1¼ cups powdered sugar
2 tablespoons cocoa powder

To decorate
white and milk chocolate chips/buttons

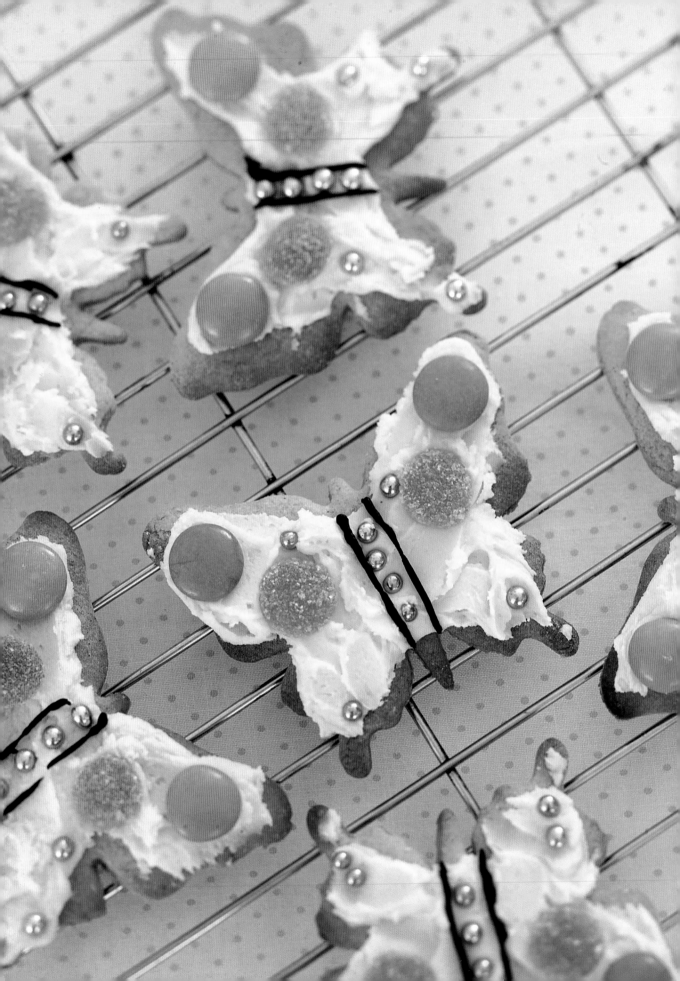

2

Cute cookies

Chocolate chip cookies

These chunky, chocolate-chip-laden cookies are quick, easy, and fun to make.

What to do

1   Help your child to cut out two large sheets of parchment paper to line the baking sheets while you preheat the oven to 375°F.

2   Place the butter and sugar in the mixing bowl and help your child beat them together either with an electric mixer or a wooden spoon until creamy.

3   Add the egg and vanilla extract and mix together again. Place the sifter or sieve over the mixing bowl, sift in the flour, and then mix in.

4   Add the oats and chocolate chips and stir in, then, using a teaspoon and a finger to scrape the mixture off, place generous spoonfuls of the mixture in 24 or so lumpy piles onto the baking sheets. Allow plenty of space between the piles because the cookies will spread as they cook.

5   Bake the cookies for about 10 minutes, until they are golden brown, then remove them from the oven.

6   Cool the cookies on the baking sheets for a few minutes before transferring, with a rubber spatula, to a cooling rack. The cookies will become crisp as they cool.

Makes about 24
Preparation time 10 minutes
Cooking time 10–15 minutes

Equipment
parchment paper • **scissors** •
2 baking sheets • **large mixing bowl** •
handheld electric mixer or wooden
spoon • **sifter or sieve** • **teaspoon** •
rubber spatula • **cooling rack**

Ingredients
½ cup (1 stick) butter or margarine,
    softened
½ cup soft light brown sugar
1 egg
1 teaspoon vanilla extract
1¼ cups all-purpose flour
1 cup rolled oats
⅓ cup semisweet or milk chocolate chips
⅓ cup white chocolate chips

Coconut racoons

These coconut macaroons have one side dipped in melted chocolate to give them a stripy, racoon look. We like these with vanilla ice cream.

What to do

1   Ask your child to cut out 2 sheets of the parchment paper to line the baking sheets while you preheat the oven to 325°F.

2   Place the egg whites in a mixing bowl and help your child to use an electric mixer or hand whisk to beat the whites until they form peaks when you turn off (if electric) and lift up the mixer or whisk.

3   Add about one-third of the sugar and whisk it in. Add another third and whisk that in, then the final third.

4   Add the coconut and, using a large metal spoon, show your child how to fold it in gently to avoid knocking the air out of the mixture.

5   Use a teaspoon to fill an egg cup with the mixture and then tip out mounds onto the baking sheets, leaving a little space between each one.

6   Bake the macaroons for 15 minutes, or until the tops are golden brown. Let cool on the baking sheets for 2–3 minutes, then remove with a rubber spatula to a cooling rack.

7   Meanwhile, melt the chocolate by placing it in the heatproof bowl over a small saucepan of simmering water. When it has melted, stir the chocolate then remove the bowl from the pan and let it cool a little.

8   Help your child to dip the cooled macaroons into the chocolate and place on fresh pieces of parchment paper until they set.

9   When set, peel the macaroons off the paper.

Makes about 20
Preparation time 15 minutes
Cooking time 15 minutes

Equipment
parchment baking paper • scissors • 2 large baking sheets • large mixing bowl • handheld electric mixer or hand whisk • large metal spoon • teaspoon • egg cup • rubber spatula • cooling rack • small heatproof bowl • small saucepan • wooden spoon

Ingredients
3 egg whites
½ cup sugar
2 cups shredded coconut
3½ ounces semisweet chocolate, broken into small pieces, to decorate

Sparkly starfish

Buttery shortbread cut into tiny stars and decorated with sparkly sugar, these little cookies make great presents stacked into a bag and tied with a pretty ribbon.

What to do

1   Help your child to cut out 2 large sheets of parchment paper to line the baking sheets while you preheat the oven to 325°F.

2   Place the flour, rice flour, and sugar in the mixing bowl and have your child mix them together with their hands. Add the butter in one or two big lumps and let your child work it into the dry ingredients with their fingers, squashing and kneading it into a soft dough. (See tips for kneading dough on page 10.)

3   Add the coloring and squash the dough until the coloring is evenly mixed through and you have a light green dough.

4   Dust the work surface with flour and place the dough into the middle. Help your child press out the dough with the ball of his hand until it is about ¼ inch thick.

5   Show your child how to use a floured cutter to cut out the shapes, then place them on the prepared baking sheets. Keep squashing the leftover pieces of pastry together until you can't cut out any more stars.

6   Brush the shapes with a little egg and then sprinkle with the light brown sugar or cake decorations. Bake for 10 minutes, or until golden around the edges.

7   Remove the cookies from the oven and let stand on the baking sheets until cool. Store in an airtight container.

Makes about 100
Preparation time 30 minutes
Cooking time 10 minutes

Equipment
**parchment paper • scissors •
2 large baking sheets • mixing bowl •
sifter or sieve • small star- or other
shaped cutter • pastry brush**

Ingredients
**1¼ cups all-purpose flour, plus exra
    for dusting
3 tablespoons rice flour
¼ cup sugar
½ cup (1 stick) butter, softened
few drops green food coloring
1 small egg, beaten
2 tablespoons light brown sugar or
    colored sugar cake decorations**

Tiny Tip

Rice flour gives the cookies a slightly crunchy texture but can be omitted, in which case use another ¼ cup of all-purpose flour.

Down-under cookies

Makes 16
Preparation time 20 minutes
Cooking time 15 minutes

Equipment
2 large baking sheets • **large**
saucepan • **small bowl or ramekin** •
teaspoon • **large mixing bowl** •
spatula • **cooling rack**

Ingredients
vegetable oil, for greasing
1½ cups (1 stick) butter
1 tablespoon syrup
1 tablespoon boiling water
1 teaspoon baking soda
1½ cups rolled oats
1 cup all-purpose flour
½ cup shredded coconut
½ cup soft light brown sugar

This recipe is based on the Australian and New Zealand Anzac cookies made to commemorate soldiers who gave their lives in both World Wars.

What to do

 1 Sprinkle a few drops of vegetable oil on each of the baking sheets and have your little one smear it all over with their fingers. Preheat the oven to 325°F.

2 Place the butter and syrup in the saucepan and heat gently. Place the boiling water in a small bowl or ramekin and have your child add the baking soda and stir it in with a teaspoon. Add this to the syrup, stir, and watch it fizz.

 3 Place all the remaining ingredients in a large bowl and let your child mix them together with his hands, then tip the mixture into the saucepan and stir well to combine.

4 Show your child how to pile small spoonfuls of the mixture onto the prepared baking sheets, using the teaspoon. Leave plenty of space between each mound to allow the cookies to spread as they cook.

5 Bake the cookies for 15 minutes until golden brown, then remove them from the oven and let cool for 5 minutes on the baking sheets before transferring to a cooling rack with a spatula.

Monkey nut cookies

These are proper cookies with a slightly dense, fudgy center and a crispy outside.

What to do

1 Show your child how to cut out 2 large sheets of the parchment paper to fit the baking sheets while you preheat the oven to 375°F.

2 Place the butter, peanut butter, and sugar in a bowl and help your child beat them together with a wooden spoon or handheld electric mixer until smooth.

3 Crack the egg and have your child carefully break it into the mix. Stir together.

4 Using a sifter or balancing the sieve on top of the bowl, add the flour, baking powder, and baking soda, sift in, and mix well.

5 Help your child put heaped teaspoonfuls of the mixture onto the prepared baking sheets, leaving plenty of space between each mound.

6 Bake the cookies for 12–15 minutes or until they are light golden with firm edges but still have slightly soft centers. Remove them from the oven and, with a rubber spatula, transfer immediately to a cooling rack.

Makes 20
Preparation time 20 minutes
Cooking time 12–15 minutes

Equipment
**parchment paper • scissors •
2 large baking sheets • large mixing
bowl • wooden spoon or handheld
electric mixer • sifter or sieve • teaspoon
• rubber spatula • cooling rack**

Ingredients
**½ cup (1 stick) butter or margarine,
   softened
6 tablespoons smooth peanut butter
½ cup, plus 2 tablespoons soft light
   brown sugar
1 egg
1¾ cups all-purpose flour
¼ teaspoon baking powder
¼ teaspoon baking soda**

Gingerbread kings and queens

Let your little one's imagination run wild decorating these figures.

What to do

1   Help your child to cut 2 large sheets of parchment paper to cover the baking sheets.

2   Place the butter and sugar in a large mixing bowl and beat until creamy.

3   Crack the egg for your child and let herbreak it carefully into the mixture. Add the vanilla extract and mix again until smooth.

 4   Sift the flour and ginger into the mixing bowl, then stir with a wooden spoon to make a soft dough. Have your child put her hands in the bowl and pull all the ingredients together into a ball. If the dough is sticky, add a little more flour.

 5   Wrap the dough in plastic wraps and chill it in the refrigerator for 1 hour. When chilled, dust a work surface with flour and help your little one roll or press out the dough with their fingers until it is about ¼ inch thick.

 6   Preheat the oven to 350°F. Show your child how to use the cutters and place the shapes on the prepared baking sheets using a rubber spatula.

7   Bake the cookies for 10–15 minutes, or until a pale golden color. Transfer to a cooling rack and let cool.

8   When the gingerbread figures are cool, decorate them using candy gems, icing pens, and cake decorations.

Makes about 12
Preparation time 30 minutes, plus chilling
Cooking time 10–15 minutes

Equipment
parchment paper • scissors • 2 large baking sheets • large mixing bowl • wooden spoon or handheld electric mixer • sifter or sieve • plastic wrap • rolling pin • gingerbread men and women cutters • rubber spatula • cooling rack

Ingredients
½ cup (1 stick) butter or margarine, softened
½ cup sugar
1 egg
few drops vanilla extract
1¾ cups all-purpose flour, plus extra for dusting
1 tablespoon ground ginger

To decorate
small candies
icing pens
cake decorations

Smiley face cookies

These double-layered cookies are filled with loads of gooey jam.

Makes about 20
Preparation time 30 minutes, plus chilling
Cooking time 10–15 minutes

Equipment
**parchment paper • scissors •
2 large baking sheets • large
mixing bowl • wooden spoon or
handheld electric mixer • sifter or sieve •
plastic wrap • rolling pin • round cutters
• plastic drinking straws • cooling
rack • teaspoon**

Ingredients
**½ cup (1 stick) butter or margarine,
  softened
½ cup sugar
1 egg
few drops vanilla extract
2 cups all-purpose flour, plus extra
  for dusting**

To decorate
**3–4 tablespoons raspberry
  or strawberry jam**

What to do

1 Help your child to cut 2 large sheets of parchment paper to cover the baking sheets.

2 Place the butter and sugar in a large mixing bowl and beat together until creamy.

3 Crack the egg for your child and let them break it carefully into the mixture. Add the vanilla extract and mix again until smooth.

4 Sift in the flour and stir to make a soft dough. Have your child put her hands in the bowl and pull all the ingredients into a ball. If the dough is sticky, add a little more flour.

5 Wrap the dough in plastic film and chill for 1 hour. Preheat the oven 350°F. Dust a work surface with flour and help your little one roll or press out the dough with their fingers until it is about ¼ inch thick.

6 Show your child how to use the cutters. Cut 2 circles for each cookie then use a straw to cut out the eyes and mouth on half the circles. Place the shapes on the prepared baking sheets.

7 Bake the cookies for 10–15 minutes, or until a pale golden color. Transfer to a cooling rack and let cool.

8 Take a pair of cookies and spread ½ teaspoon of jam on the bottom one. Place the other circle with the face on top and sandwich together. Repeat with the remaining cookies.

Vanilla flowers

Here's a chance for your child to try her hand at piping. Mastering the piping bag can be tricky but the process is very exciting.

What to do

1. Show your child how to cut 2 sheets of parchment paper to fit the baking sheets. Place the butter and vanilla extract in the mixing bowl and help your child to sift in the powdered sugar, then cream the ingredients together with the wooden spoon.

2. Sift in the flour and the cornstarch a little at a time and fold in with the metal spoon. Fold back the piping bag so that the top is halfway down the bag. Spoon in the mixture, fold the bag back up, and twist it together from the top down to the mixture.

 3. Show your child how to hold the nozzle with one hand and the twisted bag with the other. As she squeezes the bag, the mixture should be forced out. Continue to twist the bag down as the mixture is piped out.

 4. Pipe the mixture onto the prepared baking sheets in little flower shapes. To finish a flower, push the nozzle down into the piped flower as you stop squeezing. If your little one cannot get the hang of this, help her by cutting the mixture with a knife to finish each flower.

5. While your child is piping, preheat the oven to 375°F.

 6. When all the flowers are piped, your child can press a decoration into the center of each one.

7. Bake the cookies for 10–15 minutes, or until they are a pale golden color. Remove from the oven and let cool for a few minutes on the baking sheets before transferring to a cooling rack with a rubber spatula.

Makes 30
Preparation time 30 minutes
Cooking time 10–15 minutes

Equipment
**parchment paper • scissors •
2 large baking sheets • large mixing
bowl • sifter or sieve • wooden spoon •
large metal spoon • piping bag fitted
with a ½-inch star nozzle • knife •
cooling rack • rubber spatula**

Ingredients
**½ cup (1 stick), plus 6 tablespoons butter,
  softened
½ cup powdered sugar
few drops vanilla extract
1½ cups all-purpose flour
⅓ cup cornstarch
cake decorations, to decorate**

Frangipane wheels

Makes 15
Preparation time 15 minutes
Cooking time 15 minutes

Equipment
parchment baking paper • scissors •
2 large baking sheets • rolling pin •
tablespoon • dessert spoon • sharp knife

Ingredients
14-ounce package store-bought puff
  pastry, thawed if frozen, removed from
  refrigerator 15 minutes before use
1¾ cups (8 ounces) marzipan (almond
  paste)
2 tablespoons raspberry or strawberry
  jam
all-purpose flour, powdered sugar, and
  granulated sugar for dusting

These light and crispy pastries are very quick to make. They are great as a dessert too, served with stewed fruit or yogurt.

What to do

1 Have your child dust the work surface with a little flour while you preheat the oven to 350°F. Then help her to cut a piece of parchment paper to line each baking sheet.

2 Unroll the pastry onto the flour-dusted work surface and pat it down gently with your fingertips. Alongside, dust the work surface with powdered sugar and help your child roll the marzipan out to the same size as the pastry rectangle.

3 Place the marzipan on top of the pastry. Dollop the jam into the middle of the marzipan and spread it thinly all over with a dessert spoon.

4 Roll up the pastry and marzipan together to make a long sausage shape.

5 Using a sharp knife, cut the roll into ½ inch slices. Help your child place each slice on the baking sheet.

6 Bake the pastries for 15 minutes, or until puffed and golden. Transfer to a cooling rack.

7 Let your child sprinkle the pastries with regular granulated sugar while still warm.

Smarty pants

Makes 20
Preparation time 20 minutes, plus chilling
Cooking time 10–15 minutes

Equipment
**parchment paper • scissors •
2 large baking sheets • large mixing
bowl • wooden spoon or handheld
electric mixer • sifter or sieve • plastic
wrap • rolling pin • trouser-shaped
template and sharp knife (or cutter) •
cooling rack**

Ingredients
**½ cup (1 stick) butter or margarine,
    softened
½ cup sugar
1 egg
few drops vanilla extract
1¾ cups all-purpose flour
3 tablespoons cocoa powder
package of candies, to decorate**

Make a template for these cute cookies by drawing a simple trouser shape on cardboard, then help your child to cut around the shape.

What to do

1   Help your child to cut 2 large sheets of parchment paper to cover the baking sheets.

2   Help your child to place the butter and sugar in a large mixing bowl and beat together until creamy.

3   Crack the egg for your child and let him break it carefully into the mixture. Add the vanilla extract and mix again until smooth.

4   Sift in the flour and cocoa powder, then stir to make a soft dough. Have your child put his hands in the bowl and pull all the ingredients together into a ball. If the dough is sticky, add a little more flour.

5   Wrap the dough in plastic wrap and chill in the refrigerator for 1 hour.

6   Preheat the oven to 350°F. Dust a work surface with flour and help your little one roll or press out the dough with his fingers until it is about ¼ inch thick.

7   Help your child cut around the template and place the trouser shapes on the prepared baking sheets.

8   Show him how to press a few candies into each cookie.

9   Bake the cookies for 10–15 minutes, or until a pale golden color. Transfer to a cooling rack and let cool.

Butterfly cookies

Makes 20
Preparation time 30 minutes, plus chilling
Cooking time 10–15 minutes

Equipment

**sifter or sieve • large mixing bowl •
wooden spoon • measuring jug or small
bowl • fork • plastic wrap • parchment
paper • scissors • 2 large baking sheets
• rolling pin • butterfly-shaped cutter •
cooling rack • handheld electric mixer
(optional)• small bowl • teaspoon**

Ingredients

**2¼ cups all-purpose flour, plus extra for
dusting
1 dessert spoon cinnamon (optional)
½ cup soft light brown sugar
6 tablespoons butter, cut into pieces
1 egg
2 tablespoons corn syrup**

For the icing

**4 tablespoons butter, softened
1¼ cups powdered sugar
2 teaspoons milk
few drops food coloring (optional)**

To decorate

**cake decorations or small candies
icing pens**

Here's a chance for your child's creative
imagination to run wild.

What to do

 1 Sift the flour and cinnamon, if using, into a bowl. Stir in the sugar.

 2 Add the butter pieces. Show your child how to rub the mixture together with their fingertips until it resembles bread crumbs.

3 Crack the egg and have your child carefully break it into the measuring jug. Add the syrup and let them beat it with a fork. Add to the flour mix and stir into a ball. Place the dough in plastic wrap and chill for 1 hour.

4 Meanwhile, preheat the oven to 340°F. Help your child to cut 2 large sheets of the parchment paper to line the baking sheets.

 5 Sprinkle some flour on the work surface and place the chilled dough in the middle. Help your child to roll or press out the dough to a thickness of ¼ inch.

 6 Show your child how to use a butterfly-shaped cutter to cut out about 20 biscuits.

7 Bake the cookies for 10–15 minutes or until golden brown around the edges, then remove from the oven. Let them cool on the baking sheets for a few minutes, then transfer to the cooling rack to cool completely.

8 Meanwhile, make the butter icing by mixing the ingredients together in a small bowl with a wooden spoon or handheld electric mixer.

 9 Use a teaspoon to dollop and/or spread the icing over the cooled cookies. Decorate by pressing in small candies and/or cake decorations and drawing with the icing pens.

Soft blueberry cookies

These cookies are soft, scrumptious, and full of those oh-so-good-for-you-and-still-utterly-delicious blueberries.

What to do

1   Show your little one how to cut out 2 large sheets of the parchment paper to line the baking sheets while you preheat the oven to 350°F.

2   Place the butter and sugar in the mixing bowl and help your child beat them together until creamy, either with a handheld electric mixer or a wooden spoon.

3   Add the egg and vanilla extract and beat again, sift in the flour. Finally, add the lemon rind and mix together.

4   Show your child how to use a dessert spoon to pour mounds of the mixture on the baking sheets, then use the back of the spoon to spread the mounds into rounds. Leave plenty of space between the rounds to allow the cookies to spread when cooking.

5   Bake the cookies for 12–15 minutes, until a pale golden color, then remove from the oven and let cool for a few minutes before transferring to a cooling rack with a rubber spatula. Let them cool and become crisp.

Makes 12
Preparation time 15 minutes
Cooking time 12–15 minutes

Equipment
parchment paper • scissors • 2 large baking sheets • large mixing bowl • handheld electric mixer or wooden spoon • sifter or sieve • dessert spoon • cooling rack • rubber spatula

Ingredients
6 tablespoons butter or margarine, softened
½ cup soft light brown sugar
1 egg
1 teaspoon vanilla extract
1½ cups all-purpose flour
grated rind of an unwaxed lemon
¾ cup blueberries

3

Easy peasy

Chocolate scribble cake

This really quick and easy chocolate brownie-style sponge mixture is decorated with glacé icing scribbles.

Makes 9 squares
Preparation time 15 minutes
Cooking time 20 minutes

Equipment
shallow cake pan, 8 inches square • **nonstick baking paper** • **pencil and scissors** • **small heatproof bowl** • **small saucepan** • **large mixing bowl** • **sifter or sieve** • **wooden spoon** • **spatula** • **knife**

Ingredients
4 tablespoons butter or margarine
2 ounces semisweet chocolate, broken into small pieces
½ cup soft light brown sugar, plus 2 tablespoons
2 eggs
½ cup all-purpose flour
icing pens, to decorate

What to do

1 Preheat the oven to 350°F. Place the pan on a piece of wax paper and show your child how to draw around it with the pencil and then cut it out. Place the paper in the base of the baking tin.

2 Place the butter and chocolate in a small heatproof bowl. Fill the small pan with approximately 2 inches of water, bring it to a boil, then lower the heat so the water is simmering.

3 Place the heatproof bowl containing the chocolate and butter over this simmering water so that it is suspended on the top of the saucepan and the chocolate will melt slowly.

4 Break the eggs into a large mixing bowl, then add the sugar and sift in the flour. Ask your child to stir them together vigorously.

5 Stir the melted chocolate and butter and carefully pour it into the mixing bowl. Ask your child to stir the mixture until you have a smooth chocolate goo.

6 Pour the mixture into the pan, using the spatula to scrape every last bit from the bowl, then place in the hottest part of your preheated oven for 20 minutes or until just firm when you touch it gently in the middle of the top.

7 Allow the cake to cool in the pan and then cut it into 9 pieces in the pan.

8 Ask your child to decorate the squares with icing pens, perhaps drawing pictures of each family member on that person's piece of cake.

Queen of hearts' tarts

Makes 12
Preparation time 30 minutes
Cooking time 15 minutes

Equipment
paper towel • **12-cup muffin pan** •
**3¼-inch circular pastry cutter, fluted
or plain** • **fork** • **rolling pin** • **aluminum
foil or parchment paper** • **baking beans**
• **teaspoon** • **small rubber spatula** •
cooling rack

Ingredients
**knob of softened butter or margarine to
grease the pan**
**handful of flour to dust the surfaces and
rolling pin**
**12-ounces package frozen or chilled,
store-bought shortcrust pastry, thawed
if frozen**
**approx ½ cup jam (or selection such
as apricot, strawberry, raspberry,
lemon curd)**

These very simple jammy tarts will introduce
your child to the pleasures of cutting and
eating pastry.

What to do

 1 Preheat the oven to 425°F. Using a sheet of paper towel, ask your little one to help you smear the butter around each of the cups in the muffin pan so the pastry will not stick.

 2 Dust a work surface with flour and then unroll the pastry sheet so that it lies flat. Show your child how to cut circles in the pastry with the pastry cutter. Any leftover pastry can be squashed together into a ball then rolled out again with a rolling pin so further circles can be cut with the pastry cutter. Place each circle in a cup in the muffin pan and gently press it down.

3 Use a fork to pierce the bottom of each circle to let out any air. Tear up small pieces of aluminum foil or parchment paper 2 inches square. Help your child gently press a piece into each pastry shell, then fill each one with baking beans.

4 Place the shells in the oven for 5 minutes, then take out and remove the baking beans and foil. Return to the oven for a further 5 minutes, or until the tart cases are golden brown on the edges and just hardened on the bottoms.

 5 Ask your child to help you place teaspoons of jam in each pastry shell until they are two-thirds full.

6 Put the tarts back in the oven for a further 5 minutes. Use a small rubber spatula to loosen and remove each tart from the pan and place on a cooling rack. Let cool completely before eating.

Iced blueberry and white chocolate muffins

Makes 12
Preparation time 20 minutes
Cooking time 15 minutes

Equipment

12 paper muffin liners • 12-cup muffin pan • large mixing bowl • 2 wooden spoons • sifter or sieve • dessert spoon • small saucepan • tablespoon • small mixing bowl • sieve or strainer • large serving plate • teaspoon

Ingredients

½ cup sugar
4 tablespoons butter or margarine, softened
1 egg
1¼ cups all-purpose flour
½ cup milk
1 teaspoon vanilla extract
⅔ cup fresh blueberries
2 ounces white chocolate chips

For the icing

3 tablespoons fresh blueberries, plus extra for decorating
1 cup powdered sugar

If you enjoy blueberries as much as we do, you'll love these muffins.

What to do

 1 Preheat the oven to 375°F, and ask your child to place the paper liners in the muffin pan.

 2 Place the sugar and butter in a large mixing bowl and ask your child to mash them together vigorously with a wooden spoon. Help your child to add the egg by cracking it for her first.

 3 Ask your little one to sift in the flour and stir it in, but only briefly. Finally, have her add the milk, vanilla extract, blueberries, and white chocolate chips, and quickly stir them in, too. Using a dessert spoon, get you child to fill each paper liner two-thirds full.

4 Place the muffins in the oven and cook for 15 minutes, then allow the cooked muffins to cool in the pan.

5 Make the icing by placing a handful of the fresh blueberries in a small saucepan with 4 tablespoons of water and heat gently on the hob. Mash the blueberries with the back of a wooden spoon until you have a bright purple mush, then remove from the heat and strain through a sieve or strainer into a small mixing bowl.

 6 Sift in the powdered sugar and stir together to make a smooth, purple glacé icing.

 7 Place the muffins on a large serving plate and ask your child to drizzle the icing onto the tops of the muffins with a teaspoon. Decorate the iced muffins by pressing a nice fat blueberry onto the top of each one.

Crispy crowns

These crispy cakes filled with dried fruit and fruit flake jewels are perfect for parties.

What to do

1   Use a clean pair of scissors to cut the dried apricots into small pieces in a mixing bowl. Depending on the age of your child, he may or may not be able to manage this. Add the puffed rice and dried fruit and stir them together.

2   Ask your child to set out 20 or so small paper liners on a large serving plate or tray.

3   Place the syrup, sugar, and butter into a small saucepan and heat gently until just bubbling. Stir together, then remove from the heat and let cool for 5 minutes.

4   Help your child to pour the cooled syrup over the puffed rice mixture and stir it all together with a dessert spoon until the rice is covered in the sticky syrup mix.

5   Show him how to take a heaped teaspoon of the mixture to fill each liner, but work quickly because the mixture will set as it cools.

Makes 20
Preparation time 15 minutes
Cooking time 5 minutes

Equipment
scissors • medium mixing bowl • wooden spoon • small paper cake liners • large serving plate or tray • small saucepan • dessert spoon • teaspoon

Ingredients
3 tablespoons dried apricots
3½ cups puffed rice cereal
2 tablespoons strawberry fruit flakes or dried cranberries
2 tablespoons dried blueberries
1 tablespoon corn syrup or clear honey
¼ cup sugar
4 tablespoons butter or margarine

Dotty brownies

These fantastically gooey, chewy brownies are dotted with white chocolate.

What to do

1   Preheat the oven to 350°F. Place the cake tin on a piece of wax paper and get your child to draw around it with a pencil. Cut out the square and use it to line the cake pan.

2   Place the chocolate in the small heatproof bowl. Fill the small pan with approximately 2 inches of water, bring it to a boil, then lower the heat so the water is simmering.

3   Place the bowl containing the chocolate over this simmering water so that it is suspended on the top of the saucepan and the chocolate will melt slowly.

 4   Place the oil, sugar, and eggs in the large mixing bowl and ask your child to stir them vigorously with the wooden spoon.

5   When melted, pour the chocolate into the mixture and stir it in.

 6   Sift the flour and cocoa powder into the mixture. Mix this in and then pour the mixture into the prepared pan. Help your child to use the spatula to scrape out the bowl so every last bit is used.

 7   Ask your child to scatter handfuls of the white chocolate chips over the top of the mixture in the pan.

8   Place the pan in the hottest part of the oven and bake for 20 minutes. The brownies should still be slightly soft in the center. Leave in the pan to cool, then cut into 16 pieces.

Tiny Tip

If you want, add pieces of walnuts or pecan nuts to the mixture.

Makes 16
Preparation time 20 minutes
Cooking time 20 minutes

Equipment
cake pan, 8 inches square • wax paper • pencil and scissors • small heatproof mixing bowl • small saucepan • large mixing bowl • wooden spoon • sifter or sieve • spatula • knife

Ingredients
5 ounces semisweet chocolate, broken into small pieces
½ cup sunflower or vegetable oil
1 cup soft light brown sugar
2 eggs
¾ cup all-purposeflour
4 tablespoons cocoa powder
2 ounces white chocolate chips or round shapes

Soft and scrummy oat bars

This soft, buttery oat bar is made with a splash of apple juice and decorated with chocolate chips.

Makes 12
Preparation time 15 minutes
Cooking time 20–25 minutes

Equipment

wax paper • pencil • scissors • cake pan, 8 inches square • large saucepan • wooden spoon • sharp knife • rubber spatula • serving plate

Ingredients

½ cup (1 stick) butter
6 tablespoons soft light brown sugar
¼ cup corn syrup
¼ cup apple juice
3 cups rolled oats
2 ounces white or milk chocolate chips

What to do

1   Preheat the oven to 350°F. Take a piece of wax paper and lay it on the work surface, then have your child place the cake pan on top and draw around it with a pencil. Cut out the square of wax paper and use it to line the pan.

2   Help your child measure out the butter, sugar, and corn syrup into a large saucepan and then place it on a low heat on the burner for him. Stir until the mixture has melted and is just starting to bubble.

3   Remove the pan from the heat and add the apple juice and the oats, then stir together until all the oats are evenly covered. Tip the mixture into the prepared pan and help your child to use the wooden spoon to spread the mixture into the corners and smooth the surface.

4   Ask your child to sprinkle handfuls of the chocolate chips over the oat bars.

5   Bake the oat bars in the oven for 20–25 minutes or until they are a deep golden color. Be aware that they will still look very soft when they are hot but will set as they cool. Remove from the oven and slice into 12 or so even-sized pieces but leave in the pan to cool completely.

6   When the oat bars are cool, ask your child to remove them from the pan with the rubber spatula and place them on a serving plate.

Crescent moon cookies

These little almond-flavored soft cookies are fun to shape.

What to do

1   Show your child how to cut a large sheet of the parchment paper to fit the baking sheet while you preheat the oven to 325°F.

2   Place the sugar and butter in the mixing bowl and get your child to mash them together vigorously with a wooden spoon, or a handheld electricmixer if they can manage one, until they are thoroughly mixed and creamy.

3   Add the water and almond extract and stir in. Finally, sift in the flour and add the ground almonds, then gently stir the mixture together until you have a soft dough.

4   Dip your and your little one's hands in flour to stop the dough from sticking. Pick up golf-ball-size pieces of the dough and shape into crescents by rolling into sausages with fatter middles and curved ends. Place on the baking sheet.

5   Bake the cookies for 20–25 minutes, or until they are set and golden. Remove from the oven and let cool on the baking sheet for 10 minutes, then transfer with a spatula to a cooling rack.

6   When the cookies are completely cool, dust them with powdered sugar.

Makes 16
Preparation time 30 minutes
Cooking time 20–25 minutes

Equipment
parchment paper • scissors • baking sheet • large mixing bowl • wooden spoon or handheld electric mixer • sifter or sieve • spatula • cooling rack

Ingredients
¼ **cup sugar**
½ **cup (1 stick) butter or margarine, softened**
1 **tablespoon water**
1 **teaspoon almond extract**
1¼ **cups all-purpose flour, plus extra for dusting hands**
½ **cup ground almonds**
powdered sugar for dusting

Marzipan buttons

These little cookies are sandwiched with a soft marzipan center and drizzled with chocolate.

Makes 30
Preparation time 45 minutes
Cooking time 10 minutes

Equipment

parchment paper • scissors • 2 baking sheets • large mixing bowl • handheld electric mixer • sifter or sieve • wooden spoon • knife • small saucepan • small heatproof bowl • cooling rack • teaspoon

Ingredients

½ cup butter, softened
½ cup, plus 2 tablespoons soft light
    brown sugar
1 egg, beaten
1 teaspoon vanilla extract
2½ cups all-purpose flour, plus extra
    for dusting hands
1½ cups (7 ounces) marzipan (almond paste)
3½ ounces milk or white chocolate

What to do

1   Ask your child to cut 2 large sheets of the parchment paper to fit the baking sheets while you preheat the oven to 340°F.

2   Place the butter and sugar in the mixing bowl. Help your child mix with an electric mixer or hand whisk until the mixture is pale and fluffy. Add the egg and vanilla extract then beat again. Sift in the flour and stir with a wooden spoon.

3   Dip your little one's hand in flour to stop the mixtue from sticking. Show your child how to take walnut-size pieces of the mixture, roll them into balls, then place them on the baking sheets and flatten them slightly into circles.

4   When there are about 30 dough circles (which should use just over half the mixture), cut the marzipan into 30 even-size pieces and have your child roll these into balls, then put one in the middle of each cookie.

5   Take slightly smaller amounts of the remaining dough mixture and gently flatten on top of the marzipan to sandwich it. Gently press the edges together, then place the baking sheets in the oven and bake for 7 minutes.

6   Meanwhile, boil some water in the small saucepan and set the heatproof bowl on top. Break the chocolate into the bowl and allow to melt slowly, then stir until smooth.

7   Remove the cookies from the oven and let cool on the baking sheets for a few minutes before transferring to a cooling rack.

8   Use a teaspoon to drizzle the melted chocolate over the cookies to decorate. Cool before serving.

Funny faces

Makes 12
Preparation time 20 minutes
Cooking time 20 minutes

Equipment
**12 paper cake liners • 12-hole muffin pan
• large mixing bowl • wooden spoon
or electric handheld mixer • sifter or
sieve • dessert spoon • cooling rack •
2 medium mixing bowls • teaspoon**

Ingredients
**½ cup (1 stick) butter or margarine,
   softened
½ cup sugar
2 eggs
1 cup all-purpose flour
3 tablespoons cocoa powder**

For the frosting
**6 tablespoons butter, softened
1½ cups powdered sugar, sifted
1 tablespoon milk or water
2–3 drops red food coloring and/or
   2 tablespoons cocoa powder**

To decorate
**icing pens
white and milk chocolate buttons
cake decorations**

A very simple cake mix, like butterfly cakes (see page 80), but decorated to make funny faces. They were a big hit at my daughter's school cake sale and caused an excited rush to our table.

What to do

 1   Show your child how to place a paper case in each of the cups in the muffin pan while you preheat the oven to 350°F.

2   Place the butter and sugar in the mixing bowl and beat together with the wooden spoon or electric mixer until smooth and creamy.

3   Crack the eggs for your child and then have him break them into the mixture one at a time, being careful not to let any shell fall in. Beat the mixture again between egg additions.

 4   Sift in the flour and cocoa powder, then stir in. Have your child use a dessert spoon to drop spoonfuls of the mixture into the prepared liners.

5   Bake for 20 minutes, until springy to the touch.

6   Remove from the oven and let cool in the pan for a few minutes, then transfer to a cooling rack and let cool completely.

7   Meanwhile, make the frosting. Place the butter, sugar, and milk in a bowl and beat together, then divide into two bowls. Add the coloring to one and the cocoa powder to the other. Mix in, then let them set in a cool place.

 8   When the cakes are cool, smooth on the butter icing with the back of a teaspoon, then use your imagination to decorate them with a lot of different funny faces.

Chilly choc and marshmallow bars

These bars could be made by substituting the marshmallows with nuts (such as pistachios, walnuts, or pecans).

Makes 36 bars
Preparation time 15 minutes
Chilling time at least 1 hour

Equipment
small saucepan • small heatproof bowl • 2 lb loaf pan • wax paper • scissors • wooden spoon • plastic wrap • cutting board • sharp knife

Ingredients
3½ ounces semisweet chocolate
3½ ounces white chocolate
4 tablespoons butter
½ cup water
6–7 graham crackers or plain butter cookies, broken into small pieces
1 cup mini marshmallows
½ cup marzipan (almond paste), chopped into small pieces

What to do

1   Fill the small saucepan with water so that there is about 2 inches in the bottom, bring to a boil, and lower the heat so the water is simmering.

2   With help from your child, break the chocolate into small pieces and place in the heatproof bowl. Add the butter and water and set this over the simmering water in the pan.

3   While the chocolate melts, help your little one to line the loaf pan by cutting out a piece of wax paper to fit.

4   When the chocolate has melted, let the bowl cool slightly, then have your child carefully stir together the sticky goo.

5   Add all the other ingredients and stir again until evenly mixed and coated in chocolate. Tip into the prepared pan, push into the corners using the wooden spoon, and smooth the top.

6   Cover the pan with plastic wrap and let cool completely before putting in the refrigerator for at least 1 hour until it is set.

7   Turn out the loaf onto a cutting board and use a sharp knife and all your strength to cut into bite-size pieces or mini bars.

Butterfly cakes

Butterfly cakes, or fairy flips as my daughter calls them, are traditional children's party fare. Here's an easy, one-bowl mix your kids will love to make.

Makes 12
Preparation time 20 minutes
Cooking time 20 minutes

Equipment

12 paper cake liners • 12-hole muffin pan • large mixing bowl • wooden spoon or handheld electric mixer • sifter or sieve • medium mixing bowl • cooling rack • dessert spoon • teaspoon • knife

Ingredients

1 cup (1 stick) butter or margarine, softened
½ cup sugar
2 drops vanilla extract
2 eggs
1 cup all-purpose flour

For the frosting

4 tablespoons butter, softened
1 cup powdered sugar, sifted
2–3 drops food coloring (optional)
1 tablespoon milk or water
powdered sugar to dust
icing pens, to decorate (optional)

What to do

1 Show your child how to place a paper liner in each of the cups in the muffin tin while you preheat the oven to 350°F.

2 Place the butter, sugar, and vanilla extract in the mixing bowl and beat together with the wooden spoon or electric mixer until smooth and creamy.

3 Crack the eggs for your child and let her break them into the mixture one at a time, being careful not to let any shell fall in. Beat the mixture again between egg additions.

4 Sift the flour into the bowl, then stir it in. Have your child use a dessert spoon to drop spoonfuls of the mixture into the prepared liners.

5 Bake for 20 minutes, or until golden and springy to the touch.

6 Remove from the oven and let cool in the pan for a few minutes before transferring to a cooling rack and letting cool completely.

7 Meanwhile, make the butter frosting. Place the ingredients in a bowl and beat together, then let stand in a cool place while the cakes are cooling.

8 Using a teaspoon, dig out a circle about 1 inch in diameter from the top of each cake. Slice the conelike piece of cake you have dug out in half.

9 Help your child fill the holes in the cakes with the frosting, then gently stick the two halves of each cone back into the icing so that they stick up like a butterfly perched on top. Dust with powdered sugar and/or decorate with icing pens.

Chocolate meringue shells

Sandwiched together with whipped chantilly cream, these are a crunchy and creamy treat.

What to do

1 Ask your child to cut out a large sheet of parchment paper to fit each baking sheet while you preheat the oven to 300°F.

2 Place the egg whites in the mixing bowl and help your child to whisk these until they are stiff enough that your child can hold the bowl upside down and none will fall out!

3 Add the sugar in three batches, whisking in between each addition. Then sift in the cocoa and fold in with the large metal spoon.

4 Show your child how to use the dessert spoon and a clean finger to spoon about 12 shell shapes onto each prepared baking sheet.

5 Bake for 1½ hours until crisp, then let the meringues to cool completely on a cooling rack.

6 Meanwhile, make the chantilly cream by whipping the cream with the vanilla extract and powdered sugar until stiff enough to form peaks that stay when you lift out the whisk.

7 Sandwich the meringue shells together with spoonfuls of the cream using a dessert spoon, and place on the serving plate.

Tiny Tip

Make sure the bowl and whisk are completely clean and dry. Even the tiniest speck of oil or water will prevent the egg whites from whisking up to make a stiff and fluffy meringue.

Makes 12 complete shells
Preparation time 30 minutes
Cooking time 1½ hours

Equipment
parchment paper • scissors • 2 large baking sheets • large mixing bowl • handheld electric mixer or whisk • sieve • large metal spoon • dessert spoon • cooling rack • medium mixing bowl • serving plate

Ingredients
4 egg whites
¾ cup sugar
3 tablespoons cocoa powder

For the filling
1 cup heavy cream
2 drops vanilla extract
1 tablespoon powdered sugar, sifted

4

Snack time

Pizza faces

Makes 2 x 4-inch pizzas
Preparation time 15 minutes
Cooking time 15–20 minutes

Equipment
baking sheet • sifter or sieve • mixing bowl • wooden spoon • rolling pin

Ingredients
few drops vegetable oil for greasing
1¼ cups all-purpose flour, plus extra for dusting
3 tablespoons butter, cold and cut into small pieces
pinch of salt
3–4 tablespoons milk
1 tablespoon olive oil

For the topping
4 tablespoons tomato sauce
strips of bell pepper, olives, cherry tomatoes, sliced mushrooms, basil leaves, ham slices, and pineapple pieces
Freshly grated mozzarella cheese for sprinkling, plus slices for eyes if desired

It's a strange fact but children will eat almost anything that's been made into a face. I've even seen olives pass my daughter's lips, although I'm sure she'd deny it!

What to do

 1   Sprinkle a few drops of cooking oil on the baking sheet and have your child smear it all over, then wash their hands. Set the oven to 350°F.

 2   Sift the flour into a large mixing bowl, add the butter and salt, and show your child how to rub the ingredients together with her fingertips until the butter is broken up and covered with flour and the mixture resembles fine bread crumbs.

3   Add the milk and olive oil and mix with a wooden spoon, then put your hands back into the mixture and gently bring it together into a ball of soft dough.

4   Divide the dough into two and make each into a ball. Scatter some flour over the work surface and place one of the balls in the center.

5   Using the rolling pin, help your child roll the dough out to a circle about 4 inches across. Then lay the circle onto the prepared baking sheet and roll out the other one.

 6   Spoon 2 tablespoons of tomato sauce onto the center of each pizza, then spread out to the edges.

 7   Decorate the pizzas with the toppings. Finally, sprinkle grated cheese over the top.

8   Bake for 15–20 minutes, until the edges are golden brown and the cheese melted and golden.

Bread monsters

Making bread is easy and a lot of fun. For tiny toddlers you can make up the dough and let them play with it to their heart's content.

What to do

1   Sprinkle a few drops of vegetable oil on the baking sheet and have your child smear it over with his fingers.

2   Sift the flour and salt in the mixing bowl and add the yeast, vegetable oil, and water. Mix everything together with the wooden spoon, then put your hands into the bowl and draw the mixture together into a firm dough.

3   If the mixture is too dry to come together, add a little more water. If the mixture is too sticky and sticks to your hands, add some more flour.

4   Sprinkle flour over the work surface and tip the dough on to it. Have your child knead the dough by pushing, folding, and turning it. You can be brutal with it: The more work, the better. Knead it for at least 5 minutes. (See tips for kneading dough on page 10.)

5   Break the dough into 8 equal pieces and knead into balls. Make a pointy snout at one end of each ball and place on the baking sheet. Leave plenty of space between the rolls because they will double in size. Help your child to make the prickles by snipping into the dough with the tips of scissors. Press halves of raisins into the dough for eyes.

6   Cover the rolls with a clean dish cloth, then let stand in a warm place for 1 hour or until they have doubled in size.

7   Preheat the oven to 450°F. Brush the rolls with the beaten egg and bake for 15–20 minutes. If the rolls are cooked, they will sound hollow when tapped on the bottom (remember to pick them up with oven mitts because they will be hot). Transfer to a cooling rack.

Makes 8
Preparation time 30 minutes, plus rising
Cooking time 15–20 minutes

Equipment
large baking sheet • sifter or sieve • large mixing bowl • wooden spoon • scissors • dish cloth • pastry brush • oven mitts • cooling rack

Ingredients
few drops of vegetable oil for greasing
3 cups all-purpose flour, plus extra for dusting
⅛-ounce packet active dry yeast
1 teaspoon salt
1 tablespoon vegetable oil
1 cup preboiled warm water
few raisins, cut in half, to decorate
1 egg, beaten, to glaze

Cheesy feet

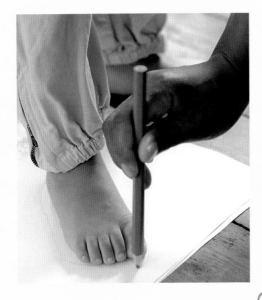

Kids will love these really easy biscuits cut into feet shapes and decorated with tiny red bell pepper or cherry tomato "toenails"!

Makes about 9 feet
Preparation time 10–15 minutes
Cooking time 10 minutes

Equipment
parchment paper • scissors • large baking sheet • foot-shaped pastry cutter or foot template (see Tiny Tip below) and knife • oven mitts • cooling rack

Ingredients
flour, for dusting
12 ounces store-bought puff pastry, thawed if frozen and taken out of the refrigerator 15 minutes before use
½ cup Parmesan cheese, freshly grated
½ red bell pepper or a few cherry tomatoes

What to do

1   Preheat the oven to 350°F. Cut out a square of parchment paper to fit a large baking sheet and place on top of the baking sheet.

2   Sprinkle a little flour onto the work surface and remove the pastry from its wrapping. Carefully unroll the pastry until it is flat, pressing it down gently with your fingers to flatten any creases and mend any cracks.

 3   Show your child how to use a pastry cutter to cut out about 9 foot shapes. Place them spread apart on the baking sheet. Even very young children will be able to help with this. (If you do not have a foot-shaped pastry cutter, see **Tiny Tip** below for instructions on making a template. Lay this template on the dough and cut around it with a knife.)

 4   Cut tiny pieces of the bell pepper or tomato with scissors.

5   Sprinkle the feet with the grated cheese, then add the pepper or tomato pieces—kids will really enjoy pressing them onto the feet as toenails.

6   Put the feet in the hot oven, making sure children stand well back, for 10–15 minutes, or until golden brown and puffed up. Carefully remove them from the oven using oven mitts and then let cool on a cooling rack before eating!

Tiny Tip

To make a foot template, get your little one to stand on a piece of cardboard, draw around the outline of his foot, and cut out.

Mini quiches

These little quiches are fun to make and can be filled with your child's favorite foods. They are great for lunch boxes and picnics, too.

Makes 18
Preparation time 45 minutes
Cooking time 20 minutes

Equipment
2 x 12-hole muffin pans • 3½-inch plain or fluted cutter • measuring jug • fork • small bowl • dessert spoon

Ingredients
vegetable oil
lour, for dusting
12 ounces store-bought shortcrust pastry, thawed if frozen and taken out of the refrigerator 15 minutes before use
2 eggs
1 cup milk
pinch of salt
4 slices ham, diced
2 scallions, chopped
5 cherry tomatoes, chopped
½ cup Cheddar cheese, grated

What to do

1. Preheat the oven to 425°F, and sprinkle some oil into the cups of the muffin pans. Ask your child to smear the oil all over the cups.

2. Sprinkle some flour onto a work surface and unroll the pastry. Have your child flatten it with the balls of hiß hands.

3. Show your child how to stamp circles out of the pastry with the cutter and place each circle in a cup of the pan, gently pressing it down with his fingertips.

4. Place the eggs, milk and salt in a measuring jug and beat with a fork.

5. Put the ham, scallions and cherry tomatoes into a bowl and mix together. Ask your child to put a spoonful of the mixture into each pastry cup, using a dessert spoon.

6. Pour some of the egg and milk mixture into each cup.

7. Sprinkle some grated cheese over the top.

8. Bake the quiches for 20 minutes, or until set and golden. Eat them hot or cold.

Money bags

Phyllo pastry is great to paint with a pastry brush, and these frilly bags are certainly tasty.

Makes 12
Preparation time 30 minutes
Cooking time 5–10 minutes

Equipment
large baking sheet • 2 small bowls • dish cloth • sharp knife • pastry brush • teaspoon

Ingredients
½ cup vegetable oil
½ cup feta cheese, chopped into small dice
6 cherry tomatoes, chopped into quarters
bunch of basil, parsley or chives, roughly chopped
pepper
flour, for dusting
8-ounce sheet phyllo dough, thawed if frozen

What to do

 1 Sprinkle a few drops of the oil onto the baking sheet and ask your little one to smear it all over with their hands while you preheat the oven to 375°F.

2 Put the feta, tomatoes, and herbs into a small bowl. Season with pepper and stir gently together.

3 Ask your child to sprinkle a little flour over the work surface then unroll the phyllo dough onto it. Peel off 2 sheets and roll up the rest for later, keeping it moist under a damp dish cloth. Place one sheet on top of the other and, using a sharp knife cut both into 6 squares, each measuring about 5 inches.

 4 Show your child how to brush these squares with a little oil (pour the oil into a bowl) and then stack 3 squares on top of one another so that they make a 12-point star.

 5 Help your child take a heaped teaspoon of the cheese mixture and place it in the middle of the squares.

6 Now for the tricky bit. Pick up the edges of the squares and pinch them together to make a bag. It's easy once you get the hang of it, but very little ones may need help.

7 Place the parcel on the prepared baking sheet and repeat with the other squares of dough until you have made 4 parcels. Then repeat with 2 more sheets of the dough until you use all the filling mixture.

8 Bake for 5–10 minutes, or until crisp and golden, then remove from the oven and let cool on the baking sheet.

Tiny Tip

Wrap up the leftover phyllo dough sheets in plastic wrap and keep them in the refrigerator until next time.

Garlic puffy bread

Children love helping themselves to this lovely soft focaccia and it's surprisingly easy to make.

Makes 1 x 14-inch circle of bread
Preparation time 45 minutes, plus rising
Cooking time 10–15 minutes

Equipment
**small mixing bowl · wooden spoon ·
11 x 7-inch shallow baking tin · paper
towel · large mixing bowl · plastic wrap**

Ingredients
**1 cup preboiled warm water
2 teaspoons active dry yeast
1 teaspoon sugar
1 tablespoon olive oil
2 x 5-ounce packages pizza base mix
flour, for dusting
2 garlic cloves, thinly sliced
1 teaspoon salt flakes**

What to do

 1 Have your child put the warm water, yeast, and sugar into a small mixing bowl. Stir together, then let stand in a warm place for 15 minutes, until frothy on top.

 2 Meanwhile, pour a few drips of olive oil onto the baking tin and have your little one smear it all over with his hands or a piece of paper towel.

3 Put the pizza base mix in a large mixing bowl and have your child add the yeast mixture and then stir it all together to make a soft dough.

 4 Sprinkle some flour onto the work surface, place the dough in the middle, then knead it for at least 5 minutes. Let your little one have a go at bashing it about but you will probably have to take over to knead the dough until it is elastic and smooth in texture. (See tips for kneading dough on page 10.)

 5 Place the dough into the prepared baking pan and help your child to press it into the corners. Scatter over the garlic slices and the salt.

6 Smear some oil onto a piece of plastic wrap and lay this over the top of the dough. Let the dough stand in a warm place to rise for about 30 minutes or until it has doubled in height.

7 Preheat the oven to 425°F. Show your child how to make dimples all over the dough by gently pressing his fingers into it. Drizzle over the remainder of the olive oil, then bake for 10–15 minutes, until golden brown.

8 Carefully remove from the oven and let cool for at least 5 minutes before eating.

Man-in-the-moon's biscuits

Makes about 14
Preparation time 15 minutes
Cooking time 12–15 minutes

Equipment

large baking sheet • **sifter or sieve** •
large mixing bowl • **wooden spoon** •
rolling pin • **2½-inch plain round or half-moon shaped cutter** • **pastry brush**

Ingredients

few drops vegetable oil for greasing
2 cups all-purpose flour, plus extra for
dusting
4 tablespoons cold butter, cut up into
small pieces
pinch of salt
6 tablespoons Cheddar or your favorite
cheese, grated
½ cup milk
1 egg or 1 yolk, beaten, or milk, to glaze

Biscuits are very easy and quick to make. They make great snacks—try these spread with cream cheese and ham or warm with butter.

What to do

1   Sprinkle a few drops of vegetable oil on the baking sheet and have your child smear it all over while you preheat the oven to 400°F.

2   Sift the flour and salt into a large mixing bowl. Add the butter and show your child how to rub the butter and flour together between her thumbs and fingers until the butter is broken up and covered with flour and the mixture resembles fine bread crumbs.

3   Stir in 4 tablespoons of the cheese, add the milk, and mix with a wooden spoon. Then put your hands back into the mixture and gently bring it together into a ball of soft dough.

4   Sprinkle flour onto the work surface and tip the dough into the middle. Gently roll the dough out until it is about 1 inch thick (it doesn't need much rolling).

5   Help your child use the cutter to cut out shapes and place them on the baking sheet. Brush with the beaten egg or some milk, and sprinkle with the remaining cheese.

6   Bake for 12–15 minutes, or until firm and golden.

Tiny Tip

To have lovely light, crumbly biscuits, the secret is not to handle the mixture any more than you have to. It's the opposite of bread, in fact, which you need to knead.

Cheesy twists

Makes about 15
Preparation time 15 minutes
Cooking time 8–12 minutes

Equipment
**parchment paper • scissors •
2 baking sheets • cheese grater • large
mixing bowl • sifter or sieve • wooden
spoon • rolling pin • sharp knife**

Ingredients
**½ cup Cheddar cheese
¾ cup all-purpose flour, plus extra for
dusting
½ teaspoon mustard powder
4 tablespoons butter, cold and cut into
small pieces
1 egg**

These little cheese straws were my first culinary triumph as a child.

What to do

1   Preheat the oven to 425°F, and cut two pieces of parchment paper to fit the two baking sheets.

 2   Help your child to grate the cheese into the mixing bowl, then show him how to sift the flour and mustard powder, using the sifter or sieve.

 3   Add the butter to the mix, then show your little one how to get his hands into the mixture and rub the cheese, butter and flour together between their thumbs and fingers until the butter is broken up and covered in flour and the mixture looks like fine bread crumbs.

4   Separate the egg for your child into yolk and white. Add the yolk to the mixture and discard the white. Stir with a wooden spoon until you have a stiff dough.

 5   Sprinkle a lot of flour over a work surface and put the dough in the middle. Children can easily shape this dough with their hands and roll it with a floured rolling pin until it is about ¼ inch thick.

6   Take a sharp knife and cut the dough into long strips, about 2½ inches thick. Help your child to pick up each strip carefully and twist it gently before laying it onto one of the prepared baking sheets.

7   Bake for 8–12 minutes until golden brown, then remove from the oven and let cool on the baking sheets.

Sunshine cornbread

This lovely soft, golden-yellow bread is delicious warm or cold with butter. It is great with soups, stews, or cheese.

What to do

 1   Preheat the oven to 350°F. Let your child smear butter all over the baking pan, using her fingers or a piece of paper towel.

 2   Have your child sift the cornmeal, flour, baking powder, baking soda, and salt into a large mixing bowl and mix them together.

3   Place the yogurt, milk, maple syrup or brown sugar, eggs, and melted butter into another mixing bowl and beat together with a fork or whisk.

 4   Pour the dry ingredients into the wet and ask your child to stir them all together, just enough to combine them into a batter because over-stirring can make the cornbread tough.

5   Help your child to tip the mixture into the prepared pan, then put it in the oven and bake for 20–25 minutes, or until golden brown on top and a skewer poked into the middle comes out clean.

6   Let cool a little in the pan, then tip out onto a cooling rack. When cool, cut into 12 squares and serve warm or cold.

Makes 12 squares
Preparation time 15 minutes
Cooking time 20–25 minutes

Equipment
baking pan, 8 inches square • paper towel • sifter or sieve • 2 large mixing bowls • wooden or large metal spoon • fork or whisk • skewer • cooling rack • sharp knife

Ingredients
knob of butter or margarine for greasing
1⅓ cups cornmeal
2 cups all-purpose flour
1 tablepoon baking powder
1 teaspoon baking soda
1 teaspoon salt
1¾ cups plain yogurt
½ cup milk
¼ cup maple syrup or brown sugar
2 eggs
4 tablespoons butter, melted

Zucchini and cheese muffins

These delicious muffins are very quick to make and simple enough for a child to do all by herself.

What to do

 1 Ask your child to place the paper liners in the muffin pan while you preheat the oven to 375°F.

 2 Place the zucchini and cheese in the mixing bowl, sift in the flour, baking soda, and salt, and mix together.

 3 Put the milk, egg, and olive oil in a measuring jug and mix together with a fork. Pour this mixture into the other ingredients and stir until just mixed. Use a dessert spoon to spoon the mixture into the muffin liners so that each is nearly full.

4 Put the muffins in the oven and bake for 20–25 minutes, or until risen, golden, and firm to the touch. Let cool in the pan for at least 10 minutes, then transfer to a cooling rack. Eat hot or cold.

Makes 12
Preparation time 15 minutes
Cooking time 20–25 minutes

Equipment
12 paper muffin liners • 12-cup muffin pan • large mixing bowl • sifter or sieve • wooden spoon • measuring jug • fork • dessert spoon • cooling rack

Ingredients
1 medium to large zucchini, grated
2 cups (8 ounces) Cheddar cheese, grated
2 cups all-purpose flour
1 teaspoon baking soda
½ teaspoon salt
1 cup milk
1 egg
4 tablespoons olive oil

5

Festive fun

Little devils' cakes

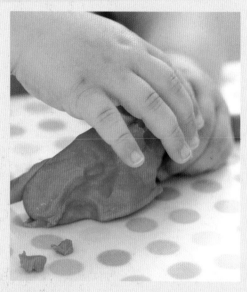

These cakes are devilishly chocolatey with little red horns.

Makes 12
Preparation time 15 minutes
Cooking time 10–15 minutes

Equipment
12 paper cake liners • 12-cup muffin pan • large mixing bowl • wooden spoon • sifter or sieve • dessert spoon • cooling rack • tablespoon • medium mixing bowl • rubber spatula or teaspoon

Ingredients
**½ cup (1 stick) butter or margarine, softened
½ cup sugar
Few drops vanilla extract
2 eggs
1 cup all-purpose flour
3 tablespoons cocoa powder
18 ounces ready-to-use rolled red fondant icing, to decorate**

What to do

1   Show your child how to place the paper liners in the muffin pan while you preheat the oven to 350°F.

2   Put the butter, sugar, and vanilla extract in the mixing bowl and help your child beat them together until creamy.

3   Add the eggs and beat the mixture again, then sift in the flour and cocoa powder and stir them in. Have your child spoon the mixture into the cake liners with a dessert spoon so they are half full.

4   Bake for 10–15 minutes, or until risen and firm to the touch. Remove from the oven and let cool for a few minutes before transferring to a cooling rack and letting cool completely.

5   Put three quarters of the fondant icing in a bowl, add about a tablespoon of preboiled warm water, and stir until you have a thick but spreadable icing. When the cakes are cool, spread the icing over the tops with the back of a teaspoon or with a rubber spatula.

6   Have your child take small pieces of the remaining fondant icing and roll them into devil's horns then stick them into the wet icing on top of the cakes.

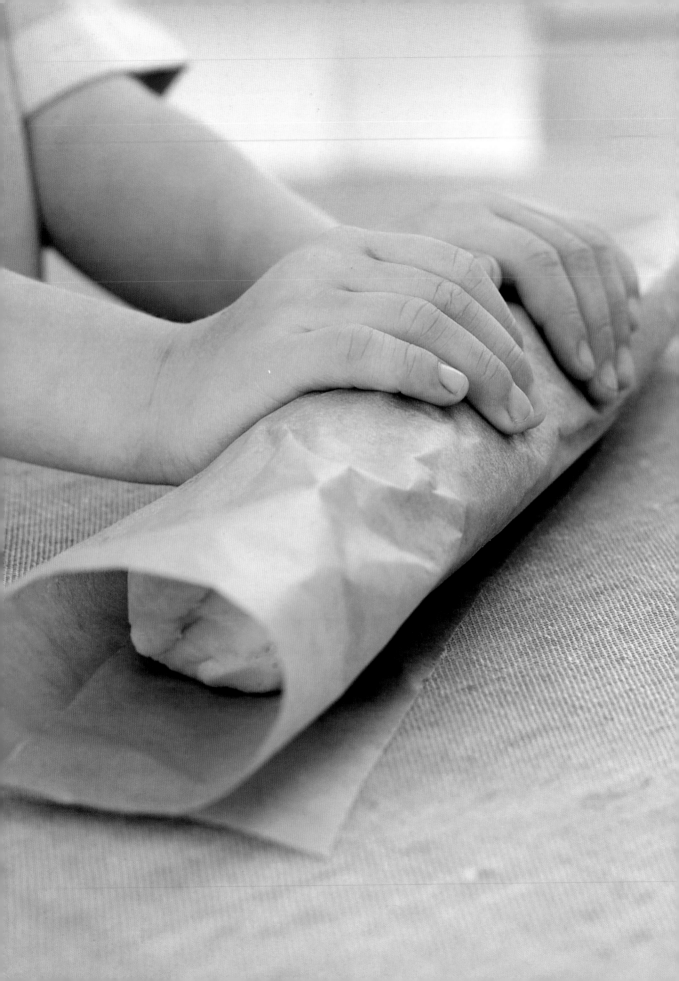

Cobweb cookies

These scrummy cookies are what's known as refrigerator cookies because the mixture is chilled until firm enough to slice very thinly.

What to do

 1 Put the butter into a large mixing bowl, sift in the flour, and show your child how to rub the butter into the flour with their fingertips until the mixture resembles fine bread crumbs. Stir in the powdered sugar and vanilla extract and have your child squash the mixture together with their hands until it comes together into a ball.

 2 Tip the mixture out onto a floured work surface and ask your child to squeeze it together with his hands and then shape and roll it into a long sausage shape. Wrap in plastic wrap or wax paper and chill for at least an hour.

3 Preheat the oven to 400°F, and ask your child to cut out a sheet of parchment paper to fit the baking sheet. Remove the plastic wrap or wax paper from the dough and slice it as thinly as possible. Place these slices on the prepared baking sheet.

4 Bake for 8–10 minutes, or until the cookies are a light golden brown. Let cool on the baking sheet for 5 minutes, then transfer to a cooling rack to cool completely.

 5 Meanwhile, make the glacé icing by sifting the powdered sugar into a bowl, then add the water and stir it in. Add more water, drop by drop, until you have a thick icing that coats the back of the spoon.

 6 When the cookies are cool, use a teaspoon to coat each with white icing. Then take the black icing pen and draw on a simple cobweb design. Draw or stick little spiders on to the webs, then let them set before serving.

Makes about 30
Preparation time 30 minutes, plus chilling
Cooking time 8–10 minutes

Equipment
large mixing bowl • sifter or sieve • wooden spoons • plastic wrap or wax paper • parchment paper • scissors • sharp knife • baking sheet • cooling rack • small mixing bowl • teaspoon

Ingredients
2¼ cups all-purpose flour, plus extra for dusting
½ cup butter, cold, cut into small pieces
1 cup powdered sugar
2 teaspoons vanilla extract

For the icing
1 cup powdered sugar
1 tablespoon preboiled warm water
black icing pen
small spider candies or cake decorations

Campfire cupcakes

These simple cupcakes are decorated to look like mini campfires. Add candy corn to make a festive Thanksgiving treat.

Makes 8
Preparation time 10 minutes
Cooking time 15 minutes

Equipment
8 paper muffin liners • 8-cup muffin pan • food processor (or mixing bowl and wooden spoon)• dessert spoon •cooling rack • sharp knife • large serving plate • teaspoon

Ingredients
½ cup butter, softened
½ cup sugar
2 eggs
1½ cups all-purpose flour
¼ cup cocoa powder

For the icing
4 tablespoons butter, at room temperature
2 cups powdered sugar, sifted
few drops orange or yellow food coloring
2 tablespoons orange juice
64 finger-shaped chocolate cookies, to decorate

What to do

1 Ask your child to place 8 paper liners in the muffin pan while you preheat the oven to 350°F.

2 Sift the flour and cocoa powder into a food processor, if you have one, add all the other ingredients, and whiz until smooth and evenly mixed. Alternatively, mash together the butter and sugar in a mixing bowl until light and creamy, beat in the eggs, one at a time, then sift in the flour and cocoa powder and stir until evenly mixed.

3 Help your child to spoon the mixture into the muffin liners so that they are each just over half full.

4 Bake in the oven for 15 minutes, or until risen and firm to the touch. Remove from the oven and let cool in the pan for 10 minutes before transferring to a cooling rack to cool completely.

5 Meanwhile, clean the food processor or mixing bowl. Add the icing ingredients and whiz for a few seconds or mash and stir until evenly mixed, smooth, and creamy.

6 Show your child how to peel the liners from the cool cakes, then take each cake and slice off the part that has risen above the top of the muffin liner. Slice this top part into two pieces and turn the cake upside-down on a serving plate so it sits on the cut edge.

7 Help your child to spread a coating of icing around the sides and then put a blob on the top of each cake. Stick the two pieces of sliced-off cake back on the top of each bun.

8 Show your child how to stick about 8 chocolate fingers vertically around the side of each bun so that they look like a stack of campfire wood.

Hot cross buns

Making your own hot cross buns together is a lovely way to spend an Easter Saturday morning.

What to do

1. Sprinkle a few drops of vegetable oil onto the baking sheets and have your child smear it over with her fingers.

2. Put the flour, yeast, salt, spices, and dried fruit in the mixing bowl and have your child mix them all together with her hands.

3. Add the vegetable oil and water and mix everything together with the wooden spoon. Then have your child put her hands back into the bowl and draw the mixture together into a firm dough. If the mixture is too dry to come together, add a little more water. If it is too gooey and sticks to your hands, add some more flour.

4. Sprinkle flour over the work surface and tip the dough on to it. Knead the dough for at least 5 minutes. (See tips for kneading dough on page 10.)

5. Break the dough into 10 equal-size pieces and knead into balls, then place on the baking sheets. Leave plenty of space between the rolls because they will double in size.

6. Cover the rolls with a clean dish cloth then let stand in a warm place for 1 hour, or until they have doubled in size.

7. Unroll the pastry and cut into strips ½ inch wide.

8. Have your child brush the buns with the beaten egg and then lay the pastry strips over them to form a cross. Trim the pastry and use the scraps for the next bun until all the buns are decorated.

9. Brush the buns once again with egg and bake for 15–25 minutes, or until golden. Remove from the oven and let cool for a few minutes, then transfer to a cooling rack and let cool completely or eat warm.

Makes 10
Preparation time 30 minutes, plus rising
Cooking time 15–25 minutes

Equipment
2 baking sheets • large mixing bowl • wooden spoon • dish cloth • knife • pastry brush • cooling rack

Ingredients
few drops of vegetable oil for greasing
3 cups all-purpose flour, plus extra for dusting
½ package (⅛ ounce) active dry yeast
1 teaspoon salt
½ teaspoon allspice
1 teaspoon ground cinnamon
2 tablespoons mixed peel
2 tablespoons raisins
1 tablespoon of vegetable oil
1 cup preboiled warm water
⅓ cup milk

To decorate
12 ounces ready-to-use shortcrust pastry, thawed if frozen and taken out of the refrigerator 15 minutes before use (you will only need half the pack)
1 egg, beaten

Easter nests

Wonderfully simple, little oaty nests are filled with chocolate eggs for Easter.

Makes 12
Preparation time 20 minutes
Cooking time 15 minutes

Equipment
**large saucepan • wooden spoon •
12 paper cupcake liners • 12-cup muffin
pan • dessert spoon • teaspoon**

Ingredients
**6 tablespoons butter
¼ cup soft light brown sugar
1 tablespoon corn syrup or honey
1⅓ cups rolled oats
mini sugar-coated chocolate eggs,
 to decorate**

What to do

 1   Preheat the oven to 350°F. Show your child how to place the paper liners in the cups of the muffin pan.

2   Help your child to measure out the butter, sugar, and corn syrup into a large saucepan.

3   Place over a low heat on the burner and stir until melted together and just starting to bubble. Remove the pan from the heat and add the oats, then stir together until they are evenly covered.

 4   Use a dessert spoon to spoon the mixture into the paper liners so that they are nearly full.

5   Bake in the oven for 15 minutes. Remove them from the oven and let cool for 15 minutes, then help your child to make a dip in the middle of each one with the tip of a teaspoon so that they look like little nests.

 6   Let them stand to finish cooling. When the nests are cool, ask your child to put a few mini eggs into each one to decorate, then peel off the paper liners to serve.

Easter cookies

This dough is quick to make and can be cut into whatever shapes you want and decorated with flair and imagination!

What to do

1   Help your child to cut 2 large sheets of parchment paper to cover the baking sheets.

2   Place the butter and sugar in a large mixing bowl and help your child beat them until creamy with a wooden spoon or handheld electric mixer.

3   Crack the egg for your child and add with the vanilla extract. Mix again until smooth.

4   Sift in the flour and stir to make a soft dough. Have your child use her hands to pull all the ingredients together into a ball. If the dough is sticky, add a little more flour.

5   Wrap the dough in plastic wrap and chill it for 1 hour.

6   Preheat the oven to 350°F. Dust a work surface with flour and help your little one roll or press out the dough with her fingers until it is about ¼ inch thick.

7   Show your child how to use the cutters to cut out bunnies and chicks and place them on the prepared baking sheets.

8   Bake the cookies for 10–15 minutes, or until a pale golden color, then transfer to a cooling rack and let cool.

9   Make up the glacé icing by stirring the water into the powdered sugar in one bowl. Tranfer half the icing to the second bowl. Adding the coloring to one bowl, drop by drop. Use a teaspoon to spread the white icing over the bunnies and the yellow icing over the chicks, then decorate with cake decorations and/or icing pens.

Makes about 30
Preparation time 30 minutes, plus chilling
Cooking time 10–15 minutes

Equipment
parchment paper • scissors • 2 large baking sheets • large mixing bowl • wooden spoon or handheld electric mixer • sifter or sieve • plastic wrap • rolling pin • 1 large and 1 small bunny and/or chick-shaped cutters • cooling rack • 2 small mixing bowls • dessert spoon • teaspoon

Ingredients
½ cup butter or margarine, softened
½ cup sugar
few drops vanilla extract
1 egg
2 cups all-purpose flour

To decorate
2 cups powdered sugar
2 tablespoons preboiled warm water
For the chicks
yellow food coloring
small cake decorations or icing pens
For the bunnies
few white mini marshmallows or other bunny tail-like decorations

Christmas garlands

Makes 6
Preparation time 30 minutes
Cooking time 15 minutes

Equipment
**parchment paper • scissors •
2 baking sheets • large mixing
bowl • sifter or sieve •wooden spoon •
pastry brush • cooling rack**

Ingredients
**4 tablespoons butter
1¼ cups all-purpose flour
¼ cup sugar, plus a little for sprinkling
finely grated rind of a small unwaxed
   lemon
1 egg, beaten
pieces of angelica and candied cherries,
   to decorate**

These garlands are fun to make for Christmas.
Instead of eating them, they could be hung by
ribbons from your tree.

What to do

1   Help your child to cut out and line two baking sheets with
    the parchment paper while you preheat the oven to 375°F.

2   Put the butter in a bowl, sift in the flour, and show your child
    how to rub the ingredients together between her thumbs and
    fingers until the mixture resembles fine bread crumbs.

3   Add the sugar and lemon rind and have your little one stir
    everything together with a wooden spoon. Add most of
    the egg and stir again until the mixture comes together,
    then have them put their hands in again and draw the
    dough together into a ball.

4   Show your child how to pick off small pieces of dough
    and roll them into ball, each about the size of a cherry.
    Press 8 balls of the cookie dough together into a circle,
    then repeat to make a further 5 garlands. Place small
    pieces of candied cherry or angelica between the balls.

5   Bake for about 15 minutes, or until pale golden in color.

6   Just before the end of the cooking time, brush with the
    remainder of the egg and sprinkle with sugar, then return
    to the oven to finish cooking.

7   Remove from the oven and let cool a little before
    transferring to a cooling rack.

Meringue snowmen

Meringues are a great favorite of ours and with an electric mixer they're a cinch to make. Children will enjoy making the snowmen shapes and giving them faces and will relish eating them.

What to do

1. Preheat the oven to its lowest setting and help your child cut out 2 squares of parchment paper to fit the baking sheets.

2. Show your child how to separate the egg white from the yolk by cracking each egg in half over a bowl and carefully tipping the egg yolk from one half of the shell to the other while letting the white fall into the bowl below.

3. Help your child to whisk the egg whites in a mixing bowl with an electric mixer or hand whisk until the egg whites form firm peaks and you can hold the bowl upside down without the mixture falling out. Add half the sugar and briefly whisk again, then add the remaining sugar and whisk again, but only enough to mix in the sugar and make a thick, glossy meringue mixture.

 4. Show your child how to use a teaspoon to place a meringue head on a baking sheet and then use a tablespoon for the snowman's body. Repeat to make 9–12 snowmen. Use raisins for their eyes, candied cherry pieces for their mouths, and give them buttons down their fronts with more raisins or pieces of mixed peel.

5. Bake the meringues for 1½ hours. For the best results, put them in the oven for an hour and then turn it off, leaving the meringues in there for 3–4 hours, or until the oven is completely cool. This can easily be done overnight. In the morning, you will have perfectly crisp meringues.

Makes 9–12
Preparation time 20 minutes
Cooking time 1½ hours or overnight

Equipment
parchment paper • **scissors** •
2 baking trays • **small bowl** •**handheld**
electric mixer or hand whisk • **large**
mixing bowl • **teaspoon** • **tablespoon**

Ingredients
3 egg whites
½ cup sugar

To decorate
candied cherries, cut into pieces
raisins
mixed peel

Tiny Tip

To whisk egg whites successfully, the bowl and whisk must be completely clean and dry.

Rudolph's Santa snacks

We have it on good authority that Rudolph likes to make these to keep Santa going through the most important night of the year.

What to do

1   Preheat the oven to 375°F, and help your child to cut out a piece of parchment paper to fit the baking sheet.

2   Put the cornflakes in a plastic bag and have your child crush them with her hands or bash them with a rolling pin, then tip onto a plate and keep for later.

3   Put the butter and sugar into the mixing bowl and help your little one cream them together with a wooden spoon until pale and fluffy.

4   Add the egg yolk and vanilla extract and stir in. Use the sifter to add the flour and cornstarch, or place the sieve on the top of the bowl, add the flour and cornstarch, and have your child knock them through by tapping or shaking the sieve. Then stir them into the mix.

5   Ask your child to wet her hands so that the mixture doesn't stick, then take walnut-size amounts of the mixture and roll them into about 14 balls.

6   Next, roll the balls in the cornflakes until covered. Then place them on the prepared baking sheets, leaving plenty of space between each, and decorate the top of each one with half a candied cherry.

7   Bake the cookies for 15 minutes, or until a light golden brown, then remove from the oven and let cool a little before transferring to a cooling rack.

Makes about 14
Preparation time 15 minutes
Cooking time 15 minutes

Equipment
parchment paper • scissors • baking sheet • plastic bag • rolling pin • plate • large mixing bowl • wooden spoon • sifter or sieve • cooling rack

Ingredients
2 cups cornflakes
½ cup butter or margarine, softened
6 tablespoons sugar
1 egg yolk
few drops vanilla extract
1 cup all-purpose flour
3 tablespoons cornstarch
7 candied cherries, sliced in half, to decorate

Mini gingerbread house

This house is fun to make, but very little ones will need help with the templates and assembly.

Makes 1
Preparation time 45 minutes plus chilling
Cooking time 15 minutes

Equipment
mixing bowl • wooden spoon or handheld electric whisk • sifter or sieve • plastic wrap • parchment paper • ruler • pencil • scissors • rolling pin • sharp knife • baking sheet • spatula • small bowl • dessert spoon • piping bag

Ingredients
½ cup butter or margarine, softened
½ cup sugar
1 egg
few drops vanilla extract
1¾ cups all-purpose flour, plus extra for dusting
1 tablespoon ground ginger

To decorate
1½ cups powdered sugar
1 tablespoon preboiled warm water
candies and Christmas cake decorations
icing pens (optional)

What to do

1 Help your child to cut a large sheet of parchment paper to cover the baking sheet, then follow steps 2–4 for the Gingerbread Kings and Queens on page 46. Wrap the dough in plastic wrap and chill it for 1 hour.

2 Meanwhile, make the templates for the houses. Take a large sheet of parchment paper and draw on it one 4x6 inch rectangle, two 4x3 inch rectangles, and two triangles, each with two sides measuring 2½ inches and one side measuring 2 inches. Cut out these shapes.

3 Preheat the oven to 350°F. Sprinkle the work surface with flour and roll the dough out so that it is about ¼ inch thick. Place the templates on the dough and cut around them with a sharp knife. Transfer each piece to a baking sheet with a spatula. Bake for 15 minutes, then remove from the oven and let cool on the baking sheet.

4 To make the glacé icing, sift the powdered sugar into a bowl, then stir together with the water until you have a thick consistency.

5 Spoon the icing into a piping bag and twist the top together down to the icing, then pipe the icing onto the house.

6 Use the largest oblong gingerbread as the base and use the 2 small oblongs to form a tent shape on top. Secure with a lot of icing along the joint (this will look like fallen snow) and let set. Pipe icing along the edges of the triangles and carefully insert one into each end of the tent to enclose.

7 Use more icing, or an icing pen, and candies to decorate the house with windows and a door. Let stand until set.

Index

Acknowledgments

Executive Editor: Nicola Hill
Editor: Lisa John
Executive Art Editor: Tim Pattinson
Photographer: Vanessa Davies
Props Stylist: Marianne De Vries
Home Economist: Becky Johnson
Senior Production Controller: Manjit Sihra

Huge thank yous from the author to her mum, Sally Johnson, for introducing her to the pleasures of baking and for her enduring support and to her daughter, Summer, for her enthusiastic recipe testing and tasting. Also to Marcus, Tash, Leo, and Lara for all their generous help during the writing process.